one couple two cultures

It's a fascinating study and long overdue for serious consideration. It's lucidly and beautifully written. Clearly a labour of love. A very thoughtful and illuminating account of what makes an enduring cross cultural marriage.

Leonard M. Cantor, Professor Emeritus
Loughborough University, UK

Your style is idiosyncratic. It's like having a conversation with the readers. Sometimes you go off at a tangent (like in a real chat) but you always get back to the point. Meanwhile the reader has learnt things they didn't expect to about life in a Chinese context. Sometimes you are thinking aloud, which is nice.

Dr Elizabeth K. Teather, a retired Australian academic

Thanks so much for doing the important research and sharing it with the world.

Kan Jansen and his American girl friend

This subject needed opening up in a non-academic way, and you have surely done this very effectively, and more. Many of your respondents have been very forthcoming and co-operative, providing you with the raw materials, and your own background knowledge and reading have done the rest.

Dr James Hayes, Hong Kong historian,
who, like Dan Waters enjoys being
in a cross-cultural marriage of long standing

Love, certainly and self-evidently, played a very major part in *One Couple Two Cultures* creation and in both the inspiration and persistence of its author. And, for these, all readers should be grateful. Not for a moment, however, does it give the impression of being laborious. Instead, it reflects several key aspects of Dan's own personality: in particular, his helpfulness, his informality, his humour, and his humanity.

Review by Sansan Ching and Anthony Sweeting
Royal Asiatic Society Hong Kong Branch Journal
Volume 45, 2005

one couple
two cultures

81 western-chinese couples
talk about love and marriage

dan waters

mccm creations

00

This book is dedicated to my Hong Kong-Chinese wife, Vera, and to all the cross-cultural couples who readily bared their souls and withstood my inquisitive probing. May we be forever like Mandarin Ducks, displaying singular attachment to our loved ones.

Let wooden gates match wooden gates and
bamboo doors match bamboo doors.

A saying of traditional Chinese matchmakers

00

Being in a cross-cultural marriage
has mostly been a wonderful adventure,
and I would do it all again in a second.

An American married to a Chinese businessman

table of contents

preface

It was such a good idea to do research on Chinese-Caucasian marriages. When my Chinese husband and I, an American, married in the United States and went to Hong Kong in 1973, I rarely saw another mixed couple. Now there are many of us. However, very little research has been done about 'us'.

An American wife of a Chinese businessman

Let me make an admission. Cross-cultural marriage is a subject in which I declare an interest. I first met my Chinese wife-to-be in 1955, and we were married on the Queen's Birthday in 1960, in what was then a very colonial, conservative, and in many ways a 'cliquish' Hong Kong. The 21st of April was a public holiday then, and on our wedding day, we attended the British Governor's Garden Party at Government House with a representative cross section of Chinese, Westerners, Eurasians, and a few inter-racial couples, including the civil servant and scholar K. M. A. Barnett and his Fujianese wife, Joan. Guests generally mixed well. Although there was a 'charmed circle', which to a large extent was self-energising and self-perpetuating, there was no outward hint of racism. Everyone knew his or her place.

In fact, in everyday life, the two races kept largely to themselves. There were 'duty' parties when the European boss invited his Chinese staff, usually once a year, to his home, but Western wives, with their many prejudices, would rarely meet Chinese of their own class, as those with whom they came into contact were mostly servants and tradesmen. This way of life was in many ways similar throughout the old British Empire.

I recall one Scottish colleague in Hong Kong saying in the mid 1950s, 'I've never had a Chinese cross my threshold as a guest; as tradesmen yes, but not as a guest. You never know what they might do!' That same government servant, having served in the Crown Colony for more than twenty years, would probably call himself an 'Old Hong Kong Hand.' Yet he boasted he could not count beyond three in Cantonese. 'This is a British Colony!' he would say. 'The Chinese should learn English.' Another British colleague was fond of saying, 'They've got to have a European behind them!' Even the author Jan Morris wrote, when she first visited Hong Kong in the 1950s, 'I noticed that Britons habitually spoke to Chinese in a hectoring or domineering tone' (Morris, 1988:67).

Not everyone was as racist as that. Most people certainly were not. But some used to let slip circumlocutory remarks which local Chinese people were not supposed to hear or understand, and these often showed a distinct lack of sensitivity to things Chinese. Yet, the Chinese seldom complained. No one wrote to the letter-to-the-editor columns in the newspapers. And, on the rare occasions they did write letters about the Government, there was never any reply.

To a large extent, the 1966 and 1967 riots in Hong Kong formed a kind of watershed. The former were largely demonstrations against substandard living conditions in Hong Kong – such as shortages of housing, school places, medical facilities and the like – while the latter were basically an overspill of the Cultural Revolution in Mainland China. The British Hong Kong Government began to listen to the Chinese population more attentively. Living conditions improved, and a larger, more prosperous middle class began to develop.

When my wife and I married in 1960, inter-racial marriages were not 'the done thing'. My old boss, who joined His Majesty's Colonial Service in 1938, told me I was letting the side down. May God rest his soul. His were pre-World War Two attitudes, and he was fond of saying, as if he meant it, 'There is something about a "good marriage".'

Although Western-Chinese marriages are far more common now, little has been written about them. While a fairly large amount of material on cross-cultural marriages is available, it is mostly about whites married to blacks , and whites to Pakistanis, and so on, and it is mostly published in the West. I embarked upon this book because I was convinced no other such project had been carried out, and that the findings would be valuable. The results of my survey are merely indicative, however. It is my sincere hope that this book will inspire further research and exploration.

I also hope that couples about to embark on the 'great adventure' of cross-cultural marriage will profit from reading it. And it is, undoubtedly, an adventure! A New Zealander divorcee who contributed to this study wrote: 'I hope to marry again one day. I would prefer another cross-cultural marriage for the interest it engenders.' Yes, the examples I include are of both successful and not-so-successful unions, and readers will find numerous comments made by the spouses themselves – far be it from me to write a 'how-to book'.

I did not aim to provide a comprehensive and rigorous account of the entire, diverse population of Western-Chinese married couples. I narrowed the scope to make it more manageable: middle-class professional, heterosexual Western-Chinese married couples. Men or women with de facto wives or 'partners' have not been included.

To gather information firsthand, I sent a five-page survey with fifteen questions to Western-Chinese couples living around the world. The Chinese people were originally from Mainland China, Taiwan and a sizeable proportion of them from Hong Kong. The Westerners were of various nationality, but primarily from Britain, and all were white. I also conducted interviews. The total number of couples consulted was 81. In fact, the sample group primarily included people who were part of my own social and professional circle, plus friends, acquaintances, and couples newly introduced to me. I am aware this 'convenience sampling' or 'snowballing technique' does not constitute a balanced sample.

Much of this book is based on oral history. To obtain reliable, inside information, many believe, as I do, that you should 'ask the folk who cut the hay.' Right from the start, I decided the voices of the spouses themselves would be the heart of the project and the backbone of the book. These are found in Part Two: Voices of 81 East-West Couples. Their thoughts on everything from in-laws to eating habits to discrimination have received the lightest of editing. To ensure they felt the freedom to reveal aspects of their private lives, I granted them anonymity. I feel highly privileged to have been allowed to listen to their thoughts and feelings on love and marriage, and to be privy to their day-to-day lifestyles. The couples were generous beyond expectation.

Part One, Voices of History, provides a macro picture of how European and Chinese men and women have lived together, or more often apart in Chinese communities such as Hong Kong and Singapore up to World War Two. How society has portrayed Western-Chinese couples in literature and the media is also discussed.

It is said the gestation period of a book is the same as for a human. For this book, even the gestation period of an elephant – over 624 days – has been far exceeded. Over the years, and the decades, I have made copious notes and collected tens of thousands of anecdotes. At a dinner party way back in the mid-1950s, for example, I was told, 'Chinese never divorce you know!' Likewise, I have heard many times, 'All marriages are made in heaven.'

The questionnaires, interviews, research, newspaper clippings, my notes, and my own first-hand experiences and recollections are all woven into this book. It has been a labour of love.

Although it could be the subject of much hair splitting, the following terms are used more or less interchangeably: cross-cultural marriage, mixed marriage, inter-cultural marriage, interracial marriage, intermarriage, dual-cultural marriage, dual marriage, bi-cultural marriage, out-marriage and exogamy. Some terms have changed over time, becoming less acceptable: 'mixed marriage' for instance is less common than it used to be.

White, Westerner, Caucasian and European are also used interchangeably. In the Hong Kong context, and in many places across Asia, the term 'Westerner' connotes a white person. Americans of European heritage are sometimes included under 'Europeans' as they were in common parlance 'out East,' up to the 1970s, and even today by some elderly off-shore Britons. The former Colonies in Asia must be among the few places where this still occurs, on occasions.

The term 'Chinese' is very inclusive, referring to people with varying customs across the huge country of China, plus Chinese living in overseas communities, and in Hong Kong and Taiwan too. This book has a focus on the Southern Chinese experience, primarily in Hong Kong.

It must be kept in mind that customs and lifestyles vary considerably within China itself and also among Westerners living in different countries, or even within the same country. The urban experience is often very different from the rural.

People and places in Hong Kong have their names romanised in Cantonese, while proper nouns of places in Mainland China, such as Guangzhou and Beijing, are romanised in Putonghua (Mandarin).

acknowledgements

a c k n o w l e d g e m e n t s

I am grateful to many persons, without whose help this book would never have been published, at least not in its present form. They were kind enough to provide considerable assistance and to share experiences and memories. I am speaking of the large number of contributions made by both Chinese and Western spouses whom I interviewed or who filled in lengthy, detailed questionnaires. Who were these respondents? They consisted largely of friends and acquaintances, but in some cases were people I scarcely knew before taking the plunge and asking them: 'Would you please complete a questionnaire?' Some couples took an interest in the project and recommended other couples. In several instances, I corresponded by email and never actually met them. In all, I have been very touched by the way many people went out of their way to assist someone whom they did not know! To each and every one of them, I owe a lasting debt. Their words form the backbone of this book.

I am also extremely grateful to many professionals: Sheron Li of the Catholic Marriage Advisory Council, Nancy Chung of the Resource Counselling Centre, and Vivien Fong of the Caritas Family Service, all in Hong Kong. I also have to thank the Social Welfare Department, as they have considerable experience in counselling Western-Chinese married couples in Hong Kong, and I learned much by talking to these experts at the 'coal face'. I am also grateful to anthropologists, Dr Cheng Sea-ling and Viky Li, who provided another slant to the subject of mixed marriages and prodded me to explore other directions and points of view.

How do young people today feel about Western-Chinese marriages? How do their families respond to them getting involved with foreigners? Here I must thank Cissy Ngan and May Lam of the Rotaract Club of the Peninsula, museum curators Josephine Wong and Chiu Hangshi, and the many young, interesting, bi-cultural and helpful adults with whom I have talked.

I am also grateful to Patricia Lim, researcher and author, who introduced a number of helpful Western-Chinese couples to me and brought various sources to my attention. Dr. Elizabeth Teather spent considerable time searching for suitable sources and gave me invaluable words of advice. I was also encouraged by such scholars as Dr Elizabeth Sinn, Susanna Hoe and Dr Veronica Pearson who, with their direct interest in gender studies, saw mixed marriage as a rich subject for research and confirmed my early view that the subject of Western-Chinese marriage had been studied only to a very limited degree. It became clear that the best person to research the subject of mixed marriages was someone 'who is in one.' I can claim around a half a century of experience.

Invariably, most researchers draw on work carried out by others, and I must thank the many researchers, authors, journalists and other groups or individuals whose names appear in the text or in the bibliography. The Reverend Carl T. Smith is an example. He has probably done more research on 'protected women' [kept women] in Hong Kong than any other scholar. I am also grateful to Amy Wong, freelance writer, and to Crystal Tang of the Canadian Consulate. There are countless others who have assisted me, including relatives, friends and acquaintances, knowingly or unknowingly, in a major or minor way.

After working on a manuscript for a protracted period of time, one can become too engrossed in it to see it clearly, and wholly. I owe endless thanks to my son, Barry Waters, and to Dr Elizabeth Teather, each of whom spent a considerable amount of time and effort working through the manuscript. Their suggestions have made this a much better book, and I am extremely appreciative. Any remaining imperfections are of course entirely my own responsibility.

I must not, however, forget to thank my publisher, Mary Chan, and my editors, Madeleine Marie Slavick and Dr Gillian Bickley. They have all been extremely cooperative and have helped me in every possible way.

Dan Waters

about the author

Dan Waters, ISO BBS was born in 1920 in Norwich, England, a city of pubs and churches. 'There's a pub for every day of the year and a church for every week.'

With the advent of World War Two, Waters accepted the 'King's Shilling,' pledging loyalty to Monarch and Country, and faced combat in the North African deserts and later in Salerno and Anzio, Italy. He was wounded three times and Mentioned in Despatches. After demobilisation, he rejoined the family building business established by his great-grandfather in 1853 and later became Managing Director, all the while studying and then teaching at Norwich City College.

In 1954, before he had even met a Chinese person, Waters joined the Colonial Service and set sail for Hong Kong where, as a member of the Government Education Department, he taught at the Technical College that has since become the Hong Kong Polytechnic University. In the late 1960s, he became Principal of the Morrison Hill Technical Institute, was then transferred to the Education Department Headquarters for planning and administration, and was made a Companion of the Imperial Service

Order by Her Majesty the Queen in 1981 for his work in education. Waters also co-authored three volumes of *Understanding Technical English*, of which Volume One has sold over a million copies.

Waters and his Hong Kong Chinese wife, Vera Chan, were married on the Queen's Birthday in 1960, and they have lived together in Hong Kong ever since.

Waters's athletics also spans cultures. An Eastern-Counties weight-lifting champion in England in his younger years, he obtained a Black-Belt in karate at the age of fifty-seven, ran marathons in his mid-sixties and holds Hong Kong All-comers records at 800 and 1,500 metres in the Over Seventy Veterans' Class.

His education also embraces his adopted homeland of Hong Kong. After studies at Portsmouth Polytechnic and Manchester University, he received his Ph.D on the history of Hong Kong education from Loughborough University in his sixty-fifth year.

His 'Big Birthday' at the age of eighty was celebrated in true Chinese style. In his vintage years, he remains active in the community. Dr Waters volunteers to sit on committees, researches local Chinese culture, gives lectures and climbs Victoria Peak. He has served as a Justice of the Peace, as Past President and Honorary Fellow of the Royal Asiatic Society Hong Kong Branch, and in 1998, the Hong Kong Special Administrative Region of China awarded him the Bronze Bauhinia Star for his work in heritage conservation.

Unassumingly an 'Old Hong Kong Hand', Dr Waters has always had a consuming interest in local history. Over the years, he has published widely about the meeting points between things Chinese and Western, such as 'A Comparison of Western and Chinese Humour,' and 'Feng Shui for Foreigners'. Before *One Couple, Two Cultures*, Dan authored *21st Century Management: Keeping Ahead of the Japanese and Chinese* (1991) and *Faces of Hong Kong, An Old Hand's Reflections* (1995).

Dr Waters jogs regularly, and is easy to spot around Central and the Mid-Levels in Hong Kong.

Author and wife, Vera, standing alongside a full-length Chinese *cheung saam* (長衫), one of several which they donated to the Hong Kong Heritage Museum. The author is wearing a *duen min naap* (短棉襖), a Chinese padded jacket.

The author's niece and her husband paying their respects and obeisances by kneeling and ceremonially offering up tea (斟茶) (*jam cha*) to the author and his wife at the niece's wedding reception. The couple are both wearing red (an auspicious colour) robes. The niece's *kwa* (掛) (coat) is beautifully embroidered, and the red packet she holds, presented by the author and his wife, contains 'lucky money' (利是) (*lai see*). Each of the gold Chinese characters in the circle with the red background, at the above back, means 'happiness' or 'rejoice.' Thus, in the picture, the two *hei* characters (囍) joined together are usually taken to mean 'double happiness.'

part one

voices
of
history

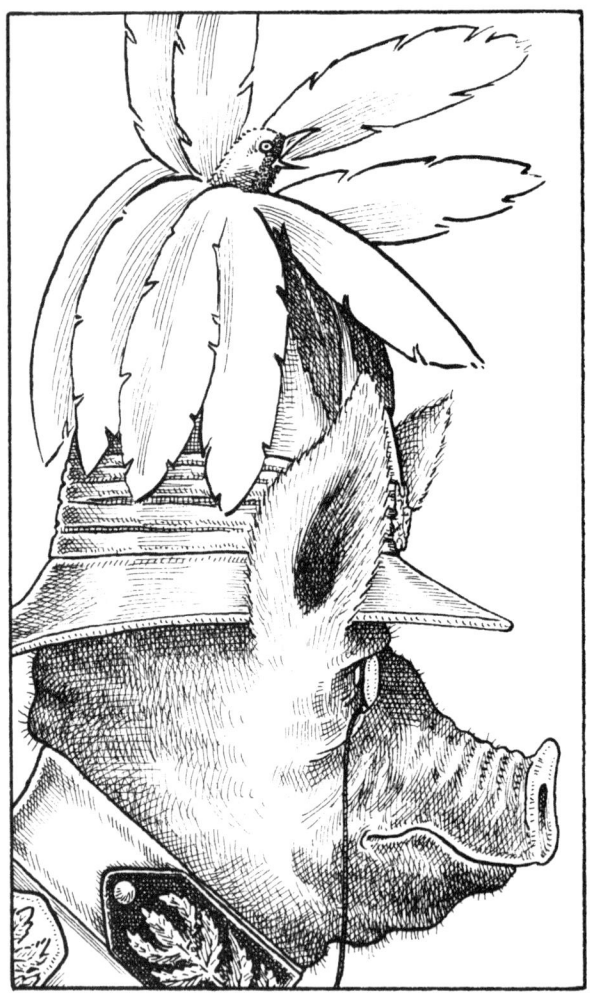

a sense of the past

Never marry a Chinese [woman]. They're steel rods
swathed in flowers.

**Journalist Richard Hughes
happily married to a Chinese woman**

Ever since foreigners first visited China there have
been cross-cultural relationships, particularly between foreign
men and Chinese women.

The Arabs came to China via the Silk Route, largely
as traders, starting during the Tang dynasty (618-906), and
people of Middle Eastern descent still live in Guangzhou with
family names such as Sha or Ma, reflecting their Arab ancestry
(Garrett, 2002:8).

The earliest authenticated records indicating the presence
of Jewish people in China date back to 718 A. D. (Chan, 1986:8).
Kaifeng in the northwest has an old Jewish community, and Zhao
Pingyu is a retired tax official from this city:

> 'I'm just like any other Chinese except that I have
> some Jewish blood. My family has lived here for a
> 1,000 years' (*Hong Kong Standard*, 1990).

A slightly built man, Zhao certainly has Chinese facial features, yet he is quick to point out his distinctively Semitic ones; his prominent nose and wavy hair, now streaked with grey, testify to his ancient heritage of which he is proud.

The Mongols from the North ruled during the Yuan Dynasty (1279-1368), and remain one of the largest of the fifty-five ethnic minority groups in China today. They are primarily resident in the Inner Mongolia Autonomous Region, a sovereign part of the People's Republic of China, and in the Mongolian People's Republic, a separate country in its own right. They have maintained their own language.

The Manchu conquered China in the seventeenth century and established an imperial dynasty, the Qing, which lasted until 1911. Originating from what used to be the kingdom of Manchuria (in today's China's North-East, or in Chinese the 'East-North'), the Manchu have largely been 'absorbed' into the Han majority. In fact, some have been assimilated so well over time that there are only a few scholars living today who can still read and write the Manchu language (Akers-Jones, 1964:43). [1] As the Chinese say, 'All rivers running into the China Sea turn salty.'

The Europeans followed, starting with Marco Polo in the second half of the thirteenth century but the main build-up developed in the nineteenth century, the Victorian times. The Treaty Ports played an important part in the history of China in that they were open to Europeans for trade and were places where Westerners and Chinese met. The earliest

[1] *Tai Fu Tai (sometimes translated as 'Minister's Mansion'), a well-preserved building at San Tin, Hong Kong, has two plaques about the founder and his family, one in Chinese and one in Manchu. This is the only plaque with a Manchu inscription affixed to a building in Hong Kong.*

of these sea ports were opened after the First Opium War in 1842, at about the same time that the British Colony of Hong Kong was established. These ports comprised Canton, Amoy, Foochow, Ningpo and Shanghai (as they were spelled at the time). Many more Treaty Ports were opened after the Second Opium War in 1860, so that by 1930, there were over forty Treaty Ports consisting of all the chief ports of China. Between 1943 and 1947, the Treaty Ports ceased to exist as such and all rights were returned to China.

It was generally acceptable in Victorian times that British gentlemen might flirt with Chinese women, although they certainly might not with the darker skinned races (Morris, 1988:55). After the annexing of Hong Kong by the British in 1841, Europeans there considered it quite natural to take Chinese as 'protected women' right up into the twentieth century. This custom also existed previous to this, in Macau.

> The climate of Hong Kong, being semi-tropical, produces unnatural fecundity. This is coupled with the fact that the men here, coming mainly from abroad, are somewhat irresponsible, the more so if they are young and single.
> Letter to the *Hong Kong Telegraph* in 1932 (Gillingham, 1983:109).

'Protected women' were so named because they were issued with passes which they could present if stopped in the street by police: the documents proved they were of 'good standing' and not the 'typical' prostitute (Waters, 1995;125).

Protected women had a degree of respectability, and the term 'spinster' (老姑婆) on a document might also refer to this identity. Believing 'unity is strength,' many resided above Queen's Road Central, including on Staunton, Peel, Elgin, Graham and Gage Streets, and on Hollywood Road. The European man bought a house for his 'mistress' in such locations, or paid the rent.

Although fictional, and although involving a Portuguese woman, a good account of 'protected women' in Macau is given by Austin Coates who based his book on the life of Martha Merop. The real Martha Merop was sold into prostitution at the age of thirteen. At the end of the eighteenth century, she was the property of the son of the first chairman of Lloyd's of London; as the *Los Angeles Times* put it, 'She came with the house.' Later, she became a trader in her own right (Coates, 1967:275).

Macau was first colonised by the Portuguese in the sixteenth century. With its outlying islands and European ambience, it has been a place visited for its beauty and relative peace. In 1849, Osmond Tiffany Jr, an American traveller, wrote:

> A man sick of the world, worn out and
> disgusted with himself and every one else,
> would find Macao a home more suited to his
> palled tastes and jaded spirit than any other
> spot that I could name (Pittis, 1997:1).

It has been said that Portuguese views towards

intermarriage possibly influenced the Chinese more than anything else (Little, 1997:118). They were certainly very open and honest about their men's relationships with local women, as were the French in Indochina. The British in Hong Kong and elsewhere in the British Empire, on the other hand, frequently subscribed to double standards. In contrast, it was not unusual in Macau for the Portuguese to accept Chinese people into their households as full members of the family. As a result, a Macanese (Eurasian) community developed which has lived generally in harmony alongside the pure-blooded Portuguese and Chinese. The Macanese also developed their own patois. Although in Hong Kong, pidgin English used to be spoken, this cannot be compared with the more fully developed Macanese pidgin (Selby, 1995:113: Tongue, 1978).[2]

A further example of 'fusion' is the cuisine. Visitors cannot really claim to have sampled Macau's lifestyle unless they have partaken of a sumptuous, luxuriously prolonged Macanese Sunday lunch. The cuisine has developed over centuries with the blending of Portuguese and Chinese food, together with the addition of ingredients and methods of cooking from other former Portuguese dependencies, such as Goa.

In Macau, where it was possible for Westerners to liaise with and marry Chinese women without an outcry, most Western men in the early days of Hong Kong were unable to be seen publicly with their 'kept' women because of the social stigma attached to such relationships. Protected women, who kept separate households, were visited in the evenings before their gentlemen returned home to the Peak, or wherever they

[2] *My amah used to say in the mid 1950s, 'I go top side,' when she meant she was going upstairs. Cantonese words absorbed into Hong Kong English include Kaifong (welfare association), yum sing (cheers! {when drinking}) and feng shui(geomancy). See also Glossary.*

lived. Many of these women were Tanka (蜑家) [Boat People], some of whom had smuggling or pirate backgrounds and spoke pidgin English. It has also been claimed that many protected women were in fact Cantonese, but the Cantonese community as a whole did not like to admit this and they preferred to identify them as Tanka who were considered a lower social class; even today, although a few Tanka have worked their way up and are wealthy, they are still on the whole a disadvantaged, illiterate group in Hong Kong.

In the early days of the British Colony, a number of Tanka women were 'aggressive' businesswomen with shrewd commercial sense. Their families provided services to Europeans such as provisioning, piloting, ferrying, and washing clothes. Tanka women were physically strong, and did not bind their feet, and in general, the Tanka were not bound by Confucian ethics as were the Cantonese and Hakka (客家) with whom, in the old days, they were prohibited from marrying. They had also long been restricted from settling on shore or from taking part in the Imperial Examinations of China (these ceased in 1905), and in essence had few ties with Chinese gentry.

The arrival of Westerners provided opportunities for the struggling, pariah Boat People to break out of their circumscribed social circumstances. The 'salt-water girls' (咸水妹) [protected women], as they were sometimes termed in Cantonese, bore Eurasian babies or adopted Chinese children. Adoption has always played an important part in Chinese society, for example, when a wife was unable to bear children, or, more especially, unable to produce a son. Because my wife's grandfather was unable to father a son by any of his five wives, he adopted a son for each wife. This was largely intended so that each son could support his adoptive mother in her old age (Waters, 1993:215). In a poor country like China, there have always been plenty of families who were prepared to sell their children or have them adopted.

Protected women's allowances from their British 'protectors' allowed them to employ servants and liberated them from much of the bondage of traditional, Chinese life. As an example, any Chinese woman in those times was subject to the 'Three Obediences' (三從): as a child, she must obey her father; as a woman, she must obey her husband; and as a widow, she must obey her eldest son; and marriages were arranged by their parents.[3]

Mind you, not all women accepted such restrictions without objecting. One of the earliest examples of 'women's liberation' were the Chinese women from the Sun Tak (Shunde) district of the Pearl River Delta – women who refused to marry or, if forced to do so, they tried to refuse to consummate the marriage (Topley, 1975:67). From the early nineteenth to the early twentieth century, these Shunde women formed themselves into sisterhoods, often went to places like Hong Kong and Singapore to work as servants, and were known to be particularly good cooks (Gaw, 1988:passim). These independent women usually wore their long hair in pigtails and were referred to in Cantonese as *shoh hei* (梳起) [combing up the hair]. Traditionally, this was only normally done by married women. But these women took part in a ceremony of their own and at the

[3] Elderly Yau Gum-giu tells the tale of how as a child of four, she was taken from her own family to live with another poor family in a New Territories village in Hong Kong. (Chiu, 1992,24) She married the male child of the family when they were both in their teens.

same time swore they would never marry.

Many of the relationships between protected women and Europeans, including *taipans* (大班) [big boss], were long, lasting and loving. When the beau of a dependent, protected woman left the Far East on retirement, his 'paramour' would commonly be placed on the payroll of his *hong* (行) [business house], where she would be known as a 'pensioner'. In other cases, the women were left lump sums on which they were allowed only to draw the interest: this was considered to be an 'honourable' arrangement, and sufficient to provide a reasonable standard of living for the Chinese woman and her Eurasian children. One doctor who departed Macau for England in 1832, set aside $4,000 for his Macanese mistress on which she was allowed to draw up to $420 interest a year (Reid, 1982:39). **[4]**

The *hong*'s serving officers would also typically look after the affairs of their retired colleagues' Eurasian children, who were brought up with the financial support of the company's salary, and as adults were often themselves employed by the *hongs*. As the children were largely brought up by their mothers, they usually took the mother's family name. I recall a Eurasian in the 1950s, who had previously used his mother's name, changing it to his English father's name because he thought, as he was working in the British Chartered Bank, it would be in his interest to do so. At the time it probably was.

That was often the case of the Eurasian child living in the city. In the more rural New Territories' villages of Hong

[4] *This currency would have probably been the Mexican dollar which was commonly used in the region at the time .*

Kong, there were two kinds of Eurasians (and locals would probably even say that this is the case today). First, there are the Chinese women who married foreigners: they have 'married out' and are no longer considered 'Chinese' by their own folk. Second, there are the Chinese men who have gone or were even born overseas and have married Europeans. Eurasian children born of these marriages, taking their fathers' Chinese names are considered Chinese in every respect. Sometimes the children are sent back, from England or elsewhere, to live in a Hong Kong New Territories village to be 'sinicized.'

Sir Robert Ho Tung (1862-1956), an eminent Eurasian who contributed significantly to the development of Hong Kong, bore a Chinese name despite having a Western father. He was knighted in Hong Kong in 1915, and he also received a total of 22 decorations from various countries. In his day, he was reputed to be the wealthiest resident in the Colony, and his family was the first non-European family to live on Victoria Peak, a 'privilege' granted largely because of his influence. At the age of eighteen, Ho Tung joined the British firm Jardine Matheson where he worked for many years, first as an assistant comprador and then comprador (買辦) [a 'middleman' bridging the gap between Europeans and Chinese], a suitable position as he spoke both English and Chinese fluently and was at home in both cultures. Ho Tung also had many other business interests, including land and property, and philanthropy. I myself remember Ho Tung as being dignified, and he has often been reported as having 'sparkling eyes.'

Sir Robert's father was C.H.M. Bosman, of Dutch descent. According to correspondence in 2002 between the Author and Andrew Tse, a descendent of Bosman, he retired to Britain where he was buried in Brompton Cemetery, in London, in 1892

Ho Tung was also well accepted by the Chinese community and, as a first-generation Eurasian, he 'went the Chinese way' in his own personal lifestyle: his family spoke Cantonese at home, observed Chinese festivals, lived according to the lunar calendar, and he himself wore Chinese clothes, usually a *cheung saam* (長衫) [a long gown] and a Chinese jacket, a *ma kwa* (馬掛) (Cheng, 1997:1). Like a typical Chinese man of his day, Ho Tung had more than one wife, and he also had a Chinese concubine, named Chau Yee Man, who is shown on the family tree. His two wives were both Eurasian; his first wife, Mak Sau-ying, who would become Lady Margaret, had no children. She herself selected the second wife, Lady Clara, who bore eleven. Within the family, the two wives were known as *ping tsai* (平妻) [equal wives], and were treated as such, yet according to English law there could only be one 'real wife', and that had to be the first wife, Lady Margaret.

Ho Tung's standing in the community must, in my own opinion, have had some effect in enhancing the standing of Western-Chinese marriages, in general, as well as the standing of the Eurasian community. The story of the Ho Tung family is told in *Intercultural Reminiscences*, written by one of Ho Tung's daughters, Dr Irene Cheng (Cheng, 1997).

During the earlier part of the nineteenth century, when disease was rife and Western women might succumb to tropical ailments especially after childbirth, it was common practice for expatriates to leave their wives at home. Many businessmen, who came to Hong Kong in their youth, never married.

Of the first eleven Scottish partners in the 'Princely Hong', Jardine Matheson,[6] eight died unmarried, two married after retirement, and only one, Alexander Matheson, married while he still lived out East.

In 1838 (some records say 1839), at the farewell dinner in Guangzhou given for 54-year-old William Jardine, who had not been home to Scotland for nineteen years, one of the toasts was 'to his health and a charming wife' (Reid, 1982,39). Poignantly, he replied the best he could hope for was [a wife who was] 'fair, fat and forty.' Although he did become a Member of Parliament at Westminster, he died a bachelor (Waters, 1990:221). David Jardine, the fifth son of William's oldest brother, is said to have written from London that, '... as a general rule I think the system of non-married partners is a good one' (Reid, 1982:39). While in Hong Kong, David had had his own Chinese 'protected' woman, Alloy, who incidentally left his 'protection' (as he himself put it) for his business rival John Dent.[7]

The Diocesan Native Female Training School, a Church of England institution and the early forerunner of both the Diocesan Girls' School and the Diocesan Boys' School in Hong Kong, was taken under the immediate supervision of the Anglican Bishop in 1868 and renamed the 'Diocesan Home and Orphanage' in September 1869. This was after it was found that many of the girls, who were educated in the English language and Western ways, found comfortable situations as mistresses of Western residents (Welsh 1993:220). Yet the 'protected woman' system continued to flourish.

[6] No merchant house has earned greater renown than the British firm Jardine Matheson. It was founded in 1832 in Canton, nine years before the founding of Hong Kong. The firm still bears the names of its two founders. It remains today one of the foremost business concerns (Bard, 1993:65).

[7] Dent and Co was another prominent merchant house founded in Canton. It moved to Hong Kong when the British first occupied the territory. It was unable to withstand the serious commercial depression of 1867 and failed because of fierce competition with Jardine Matheson (Bard, 1993:57).

With the invention of the steamship, the opening of the Suez Canal, and living conditions improving in the colonies, British wives were coming out East to places like Singapore, Malaya and other parts of the Empire, in greater numbers (Endacott, 1958:passim). The wives were colloquially, and occasionally known in English as *memsahib*, borrowing the Hindi word for a white woman in colonial India. With this development, what had been relatively amiable though unequal, inter-racial relationships between European men and local woman tended now to be replaced with a spirit of aloofness and segregation. Some have suggested this was a direct ploy by white women, the highest in the pecking order, to keep their men away from local women, although it is true there was a purity movement gathering force in Britain which aimed to halt the 'decline of the British race.' The practice of keeping 'protected women' diminished, but certainly did not die out.

Carl T. Smith, a historian based in Hong Kong and Macau, has researched the topic of Chinese mistresses extensively. In one of his papers, 'Ng Akew, one of Hong Kong's "protected women",[8] he relates that Ng Akew's 'protector' was James Bridges Endicott, captain of a ship of the American firm Russell and Company (Smith, 1995:266). Endicott bought the Tanka woman in Guangzhou and had several children with her. Described as shrewd and intelligent, Ng was a trader in opium, and when one consignment was seized by pirates, she visited their lair and threatened them with vengeance from her foreign friends. After issuing two warnings, she was compensated

[8] *Russell and Co. was one of the oldest American trading companies in China (Bard, 1993:82). It was taken over by Shewan & Co, an English firm, in 1891, later to become Shewan, Tomes and Co.*

with cargoes of betel nuts and ships containing cotton, cloth dyestuff and victuals. Endicott ended the relationship with Ng Akew when Anne Russell arrived in Hong Kong from London as a 'mail order bride.' The two were married in 1852, and a deed of trust was executed for Ng, which included property for her and her ten-year old son. Ng Akew continued in business but lived a lifestyle beyond her means. She was eventually declared bankrupt.

There is no doubt that some Chinese women are extremely tough. Perhaps the author Richard Hughes[9] could have had someone like Ng Akew in mind when he used to utter one of his favorite expressions: 'Never marry a Chinese [woman]! They're steel rods swathed in flowers.'

Many protected women in the past found that their liaisons with foreigners created opportunities. Some engaged in businesses such as real estate and money lending. One such Hong Kong Eurasian family, that is still well known today, bought and trained girls to serve as mistresses. Other women also bought and sold girls for prostitution and invested in brothels, which existed in the Crown Colony of Hong Kong as government-licensed premises up until the early 1930s.[10] Some women owned 'nurseries' of purchased Tanka children. Other youngsters were kidnapped. Even today, one occasionally hears tales of how girls are mesmerized or drugged, and then taken away to work in bordellos or elsewhere (Waters, 1995:128).

Prostitution is often considered leniently by Chinese

[9] The late Richard Hughes, an Australian, the doyen of journalists and a jovial personality, lived and worked in the Far East for many years. If he committed a slip nothing brought him to heel more quickly than a word from his beloved Chinese wife, Anne.

[10] Chinese, Japanese and European women were all employed in brothels. But there was strict segregation between brothels frequented by Europeans and those used by Chinese. On one occasion, a brothel keeper was fined HK$100 for allowing a Chinese person to use a European brothel (Waters, 1995:128).

and is sometimes viewed as a necessary evil. 'How can you blame a man for finding a woman if he has no wife to "serve" him?' is a not uncommon remark. Some Chinese have even postulated that prostitution is a convenient, low-status occupation for 'surplus' women and, as a result, it is suggested they should not be treated as social outcasts or 'fallen women', as is common in the West. Some prostitutes in Chinese communities became respectable concubines.

It is recorded that Sir John Bowring, Governor of Hong Kong from 1854-1859, expressed his concern for children resulting from these liaisons, in these words:

> 'A large population of children by native mothers and foreigners of all classes is beginning to ripen into a dangerous element on the dung-hill of neglect. They seem wholly uncared for' (Waters, 1995: 128).

This phenomenon was brought about, not so much by the protected women of the taipans, but in many cases by soldiers and sailors who had left the armed forces and had 'gone bush'. In some instances, more senior staff had also 'gone native', often together with the opium pipe. What Bowring was referring to can be likened, to a degree, to the Amerasians left behind by American servicemen from the more recent Vietnam War which pricked the conscience of the United States (Davis, 1993).[1] In fact in Hong Kong, right up to the end of the 1960s, expatriate civil servants were always supposed to be 'seen off' when they left on long leave to make sure they actually left the colony. Such regulations were

[1] *The Welfare League for Hong Kong Eurasians was set up in 1929 after an anonymous donation of HK$10,000 was received. It is a recognized charity and provides assistance to all Eurasians, not just members of the League.*

to ensure that they did not form strong attachments to the Territory, that is, they did not 'go native' and perhaps marry a local woman. No expatriate civil servant up to the end of the 1960s could buy property in Hong Kong.

Nevertheless, a few Europeans did form strong links with the Colony and raised Eurasian families, some of whom who lived very comfortably. Hector MacLean, a Scot and a partner in Jardine in 1849, was the father of Eurasian Mak Sau-ying, the first wife of Sir Robert Ho Tung. MacLean died in the Colony in 1894, after having lived in Hong Kong for over forty years during which time, so it is recorded, he returned to England only once.[12] He is buried in a special section of the Hong Kong Protestant Cemetery, reserved only for Europeans who had lived in Hong Kong for over twenty years (Hong Kong's 'corner of a foreign field that is forever England'[13])[14] As a mark of filial respect, provision was made in Eurasian Sir Robert Ho Tung's will, even though the 'Grand Old Man' died six decades later, in 1956, for flowers to be placed every year on MacLean's grave at Easter and Christmas.[15]

The arrival in the East of far greater numbers of European wives tended to divide the colonial community. There was increasing interest in status. This affected the Chinese, the European small-shop keepers and the lower ranks in the armed forces alike: they were all kept firmly in their place. Sid Coombes, who served in Hong Kong in the late 1930s, complained that the ordinary British soldier was treated very much like an inferior being by the taipan society. All the beautiful places in the Colony

[12] *Few Europeans continued living in Hong Kong after retirement. When someone like MacLean stayed on, it was often said it was because there was a 'woman behind the scenes'.*

[13] [14] *Poem, The Soldier, by Rupert Brooke. One has to live in the Territory for twenty years to become an 'Old Hong Kong Hand'. Not until the early 1970s, the Cemetery was known as 'the Colonial Cemetery'.*

[15] *Flowers are also placed on the grave of Frederick Stewart (1836-1889), a Scot at Easter and Christmas. He was Ho Tung's teacher at the Central School, since renamed Queen's College (Bickley, 1997:8). Teachers were greatly respected.*

were out of bounds to non-commissioned troops, such as the Peak, most of Happy Valley, Repulse Bay, and all the top hotels. On the Peak Tram, there was a small brass plaque instructing non-commissioned troops where to sit. In Sid Coombes own words, 'Apartheid!' (Bruce, 1987).

Among civilians, there was stuffiness and squabbling over seating in the Anglican Saint John's Cathedral, the established church. 'Do you reside on the Peak, or are you single and live in Kowloon?' was a not uncommon, pointed question. One woman was said to boast proudly that she knew no one living below May Road, which was half way up the Peak. Snobbishness was common among men as well, and the Hong Kong Governor at this time, Sir Cecil Clementi, was critical of the exclusivity of some of the clubs and took the revolutionary step, in 1926, of proposing that the Hong Kong Club be replaced by one in which both British and Chinese would be welcome (Gillingham, 1983:46). It was long after World War Two that such a proposal slowly came into effect. One British member said that when he joined the Club in the early 1960s, there were still only two non-European members. Both were Eurasian. One was the late Oswald Cheung, a prominent Hong Kong lawyer and personality who was later knighted.

Before World War Two, marriages between Europeans and Chinese were soundly condemned by the *taipan* class, that breed of men who headed the *hongs*; people who disregarded such 'rules' would find themselves out of a job. 'There are things that are done, and there are things that are not done.'

This 'rule' was even more firmly established after the British wives arrived, when Western men who did wed Chinese were generally ostracized by genteel, European society. Neither did an Anglo-Chinese marriage mean acceptance for Europeans into upper-class Chinese society. A European marrying a Chinese woman became automatically marginalised. A minority, mixed-marriage group thus gradually formed, the husbands consisting mainly of Europeans employed at supervisory or equivalent level.[16] There was no culture in Hong Kong such as that which allowed Westerners to become full members of Pacific Island or American Indian communities.

The 'kissing and merging' of two great civilisations never really got under way in any case, but it certainly took a backward step with the arrival of the white woman, most of whom, because of their background, did not appreciate the 'greatness' of Chinese culture.[17] Many Europeans still kept local, protected women. This raised in the wives' minds the irritating suspicion that many Britons actually preferred Chinese women. Eventually, in 1909, the Colonial Office in London officially forbade this 'gravely improper conduct' of keeping protected women and sent out a circular to all dependent territories, not that sending the circular made that much difference. Life in many of the colonies remained very much a man's world. The 'Morals Dispatch' or the 'Concubine Circular' stated:

> It was not possible for any member of the
> administration to countenance such practices
> without lowering himself in the eyes of the natives

[16] Although there were no official regulations in the Shanghai Municipal Police, for example, which forbade European officers marrying local women, they were not only looked down upon, but marriage allowances were sometimes refused (Bickers, 2003:151).

[17] For instance, it was perhaps not widely appreciated that China had developed a 'mature' language, comprising words of philosophy and historical research, 1,000 years before the birth of Christ (Karlgren, 1923:2).

*and diminishing his authority... it is his duty to set
an honourable example to all with whom he comes
into contact.*

Interestingly, when the circular was issued, Sir Frederick Lugard was the Governor of Hong Kong, a man who once said that the sex drive was the most potent force of his life (Waters, 1995:124). And in fact, the Chinese word for 'sex' (性) combines the characters 'heart' (心) and 'life' (生).

Many European men in the colonies continued to keep protected women, while some soldiers and sailors in the British armed forces took 'temporary wives' as if in keeping with the saying, 'Always try the local beer and the local women.' Similar 'arrangements' existed in places like Singapore and elsewhere (Bruce, c. early 1990s). Known in army slang as 'dahnomers' [downhomers], these women would live in simple cubicles in Hong Kong; the going rate in the 1930s was to be provided with HK$5 a week, a little less than one-third of a pound (Waters, 1995:135). The serviceman would visit his downhomer in the afternoon to 'pluck the fragrant buds' but was not allowed to sleep out of barracks at night. The downhomer would do his washing, ironing and other chores.

Records have it that 'temporary wives' in Hong Kong were loyal and dedicated to their men (Bruce, c. early 1990s). During the fighting against the Japanese, in December 1941, the 'Angels of Wan Chai' supplied their men with food and drink, and sheltered and comforted the wounded. When the the Japanese marched the soldiers off to prison camp, the women lined the route and cried. Although food was in short supply during the occupation, there were cases of these women putting food through the perimeter fence of the camps where 'their' men were held prisoner. If caught, the Japanese treated them abominably: one woman was stripped naked and made to stand by the prison fence for five hours in mid-winter to suffer the stares of men, although several of the European prisoners-of-war refused to look. She was 'touched up'[18] by some Japanese soldiers when they came off duty, while others threw cold water over her.

The practice of taking 'temporary wives' continued on a much reduced scale after World War Two. One Cantonese language teacher at the Hong Kong University used to take his mature European students, who were in Hong Kong on generous expatriate terms, on 'cultural familiarisation' visits as part of their 'education'.[19] The students were taken to Chinese dance halls, where no alcohol was served, only Chinese tea, but where girls could be 'bought out'.[20] A few of the girls were prepared to enter into 'arrangements' to become temporary wives.

Streetwalkers in the Colony in the 1950s, in places like Wan Chai, charged as little as HK$10 for 'a short time'. In fact, in the late 1940s and the early 1950s, when there was the scramble to get out of China with the introduction of communism, one sometimes ran into the odd streetwalker even in the vicinity of 'posh' areas of town, such as Statue Square in the heart of Central District.

[18] The equivalent term for 'touched up' in American English is 'felt up'.

[19] Before World War Two, Government Administrative Officers were sent to Canton to learn the language. In the mid-1950s, they were sent to Macau. Professional officers in the 1950s were given a language allowance and engaged a part-time, private tutor.

[20] Some Chinese dance halls did not like to admit Europeans, as sometimes they were unruly and 'could not exist without beer'. Also, Chinese clients often did not like Chinese girls who had mixed with Europeans.

Before World War Two, only in a few instances did members of the armed forces marry their Chinese girlfriends. One Hong Kong Eurasian, however, told me that his father, a gunner in the Royal Artillery, married his 'illiterate Chinese mother' (the son's words), in 1936. His father had served on Mount Davis during the Japanese attack and was imprisoned during the Occupation. The son was sometimes given the task by his mother of passing food parcels through the prison fence, even though food was in terribly short supply. Japanese were generally fond of children and consequently they were treated better than adults. At the end of the war, the father was repatriated to England and, not long after that, the marriage allowances stopped coming for the son and mother, who had to bring up the family in Hong Kong alone. The British armed forces, as well as the United States Armed Forces, did not encourage mixed marriages, believing they were safeguarding the interests of the men. He said, 'Mum was a real brick.'

After the son grew up, he sailed to England and tried to trace his father. He searched through telephone directories and sent out letters and questionnaires. He received few replies. 'You are wasting your time, son,' his mother told him, 'Your father's simply not worth it.' 'I wanted nothing from my father,' he told me in a conversation in 1990. 'I only wanted to trace my roots.'

There were also cases of Chinese men having European concubines. This was seen as exotic and special. While some wealthy men collected art treasures, others collected women. Tin magnate and businessman, Eu Tong-sen, had many business interests including Chinese medicine, in places like Malaya and Singapore, and over time, he developed a liking for the British Crown Colony of Hong Kong (Go, 2003:197). With his superb dress, including his customary silk handkerchief peeking out of his top pocket, he presented a striking figure. He led a life of luxury, including collecting antiques, drinking French wines, and his penchant for 'things' Western extended to women, too. All told, he had four European concubines and a number of Chinese 'wives' and he fathered thirteen sons and eleven daughters (Waters, 1989:6).

Eu was advised by a soothsayer that if he wanted to live a long, prosperous life he must continue building, and by the time he died, in 1941, he had built several homes in south-east Asia, and three fantasy homes in Hong Kong, all now demolished. 'Sirmio', an old world, rambling, English-style country mansion once stood on the north shore of Tolo Harbour while the other two were both castle-like mansions: 'Euston' on Bonham Road, and 'Eucliffe' at Repulse Bay. With a stretch of the imagination, one can visualise Eu's four European concubines, all of different nationalities so it was said, wandering around among exotic objects, including the splendid, extensive collection of nudes in oils on the first floor.[21] No doubt Mr. Eu had his problems trying to keep such a large number of wives happy. I remember being told in earnest by a Chinese man with more than one wife: 'You cannot take a present home for just one wife, you know. The others will be jealous.'

Ho Kom-Tong (Kom sometimes romanised as Kam

[21] *Information given by an academic colleague, the late Kwan Yim-chor at a party at Eucliffe in 1955. I was told that four wives were 'Europeans' but have sometimes wondered if any of them were Eurasian.*

(甘) (1866-1950), a rich entrepreneur, philanthropist and a community leader, like his older step-brother Sir Robert Ho Tung, had more wives than Eu.[22][23] One of them, a Miss McClymont, was reputed to be the daughter of a European tea merchant Archibald McClymont (1846-1889) who worked for Jardine Matheson (Hall, 19 2:121). Her mother may have been a Parsee Eurasian (Tse, 2003:49). Ho was said to have fathered thirty children, and every time he took a new concubine, he gave his first wife an expensive piece of jewellery. He had his own sedan chair and bearers, with their own distinctive livery, as did many well-off Hong Kong residents at that time; he probably also had a motor car at some stage.[24] When he visited North America between the two World Wars, he was welcomed with a newspaper headline, 'Here comes the man with twenty wives!' This was an exaggeration, for he had only twelve concubines, plus some other 'kept women'.

Anyway, there were many more than could be accommodated in the splendid Kom Tong Hall (colloquially known as *Tai Uk*, or big house), on Castle Road just above Caine Road. Consequently, some concubines lived higher up in Mid-Levels in an even larger home known as *Sai Uk* (細屋) (small house) at 29 Conduit Road (since demolished). The names, 'Small House' and 'Big House', did not relate to size but to importance. The typical day of the 'master' was to visit his concubines after work, go to Kom Tong Hall for his evening meal, and then go up the hill again to *Sai Uk* to spend the night with one of his concubines. At the time of writing, Kom Tong Hall is being converted into the Sun Yat-sen

[22] Royal Asiatic Society Hong Kong Branch lecture, 12 December 2003, by Andrew Tse.

[23] Chinese do not have an equivalent term for step-brother. All children who have one common parent are considered brothers and sisters.

[24] Kom Tong Hall was built (1914-1917) as a family home with top grade materials and workmanship. The architect was A. C. Little of Little, Adam and Wood, of London. The Hall was taken over by the American Church of Jesus Christ of Latter-Day Saints (the Mormons) in 1959.

Museum.

It has been written in more than one historical account, yet there is some disagreement, that one of the daughters of Ho's last mistress was Grace Pak-Yung, (a Russian Eurasian who lived in Shanghai, but who was never accepted as a concubine although she did receive an allowance). Against Ho's wishes, Grace married the Cantonese opera star, Lee Hoi Chuen (Tse, 2003:89), and they had five children, one of whom was said to be Bruce Lee.

One frequently hears that there was a favourite concubine in a family. As might be expected, she was usually young and pretty. One is reminded here of the Emperor's method of selecting which concubine he wanted to sleep with that night. At a gathering in the afternoon, he would offer a cup of tea to the 'lucky' lady. While in many families, we are told, wives generally got along fairly well together, in other cases this was certainly not so. Jealousy was a typical cause of friction. A few well-to-do Chinese, who had say three or four 'wives', might build self-contained wings to their homes so that each wife could live to some degree on her own. When there were several concubines, some must have been 'neglected' by the master and this gave rise to tales of lesbian relationships – the Cantonese term for lesbians 'grinding the bean curd' (磨豆腐), comes from dildos, which were made of expandable raw silk or filled with bean curd (Waters, 1995:95). One also occasionally heard years ago that neglected concubines were looking for 'underground' boyfriends, but in most conservative Chinese households, wives were pretty well chaperoned.

As a matter of interest, this was the first private house in Hong Kong to have a lift although this was not added until the 1920s.

Concubines existed in all walks of life. In the now demolished mansion on Conduit Road, which was built as a private dwelling in 1911, and later housed the Foreign Correspondents' Club from 1951 to 1961, the master bedroom had four bell-pulls, which were connected to the bedrooms of four concubines.[25] When I lived in a block of government flats at King's Park in Kowloon in the mid-1960s, I recall a cookboy who had two wives, both of whom were *amahs*. I also remember a wife who, when she found out her husband had a concubine, insisted that the woman come to live with the family where the wife could keep an eye on her, but the concubine was made to live with the servants. When the *keet faat* (結髮) [principal wife] died years later, the *tsip tze* (妾 侍) [concubine] became the *tin fong* (填房) [replacement wife, literally fill the room]. She was then brought out of the servants' quarters to live as a rightful member of the family.

Nearly all of the many Chinese men who went abroad to work did so alone. Many left a wife and a family back in southern China, and for the 'Southern Ocean Chinese' (南洋) who left to work in such countries as Malaya, the Philippines and Thailand, these so-called Nanyang (Naam Yeung in Cantonese) men often took a second wife and raised another family in their adopted country. Again, among the Chinese, polygamy was very much to the fore, no matter whether at home or overseas.

Moving to work and live in a Western society was another experience. In the early days, Chinese people were frequently not easily accepted, as immigration history over the past century or so shows. Historically, some Western countries enacted legislation to make marriage between Asians and Westerners illegal. One such nation is the United States. Legislation varied from state to state, but in all, twenty states enacted miscegenation laws in the 1880s, with fourteen of them prohibiting marriage between whites and Asians, and most being in the West and South, which remain the most conservative parts of the country. Some states merely declared the marriage null and void and any children illegitimate. In others, there were fines or jail terms, even a fine for the minister or priest who conducted the wedding ceremony. The Oriental Exclusion Act of 1882 further banned the immigration of Chinese: only Chinese diplomats, merchants, teachers and students were allowed to enter the country. This law was not repealed until 1943 when China and the United States were allies in World War Two, and miscegenation laws were not declared completely null and void until as late as 1967. Because of the strong anti-Chinese feeling, most Chinese people naturally lived together in their Chinatowns, and marriages between Caucasians and Chinese were very much the exception in the United States until after World War Two.

Canada was not exempt from such racist legislation. In 1907, British Columbia formed its Asiatic Exclusion League and imposed a racially biased head tax on Chinese from 1885 to 1923. In 1903, this amounted to C$500 per Chinese (Waters, 1995:84). In more recent years, the picture has completely changed and, especially in the run-up to 1997, a large number of Hong Kong Chinese emigrated to Canada. It would be interesting to see statistics of cross-cultural marriages since then.

California was known to the Chinese as 'Old Golden Mountain' (舊金山) but, in 1851, with the discovery of gold in Australia, they began to turn their attention to 'New Golden Mountain'. Life there for the Chinese was by no means easy where in many places a common 'sport' on a Sunday afternoon for the somewhat lawless European miners was to go out and tease the Chinese with their pig-tails. The gold-fields attracted a large number of Chinese and, as a result, resistance built up against Asian immigration, Australia was determined to keep the Chinese out where a 'White Australia Policy' persisted. Nevertheless, no laws appear to have been enforced forbidding marriage between Anglo-Australians and Chinese (Lowenstein, 2005:1).

In 1975, Australia introduced new immigration laws which abolished the preferential treatment of Britons and made it easier for Asians to enter the country. With strong anti-Chinese sentiments in Australia, obviously there were relatively few Western-Chinese marriages.

Legislation against miscegenation was never enacted in Britain, where racial prejudice and class discrimination probably kept the races apart and prevented most British men from taking Chinese wives. In the early days, there may have been more connections between Chinese men and British women, particularly younger women. Although not a criminal offence, two cases of sexual liaisons between 'Chinamen' and white English teenagers were viewed with a special revulsion by mainstream British society. To a Chinese person, these relationships probably seemed perfectly natural: in those days, the marriageable age for a Chinese woman was fifteen or sixteen. The Government Commission of Enquiry of 1910-1911 made it clear that there was no sexual coercion, yet it concluded, 'Such liaisons were undesirable, from an English point of view.' A year earlier, as previously noted, the 'Morals Dispatch' had been circulated by the Colonial Office, forbidding the taking of local concubines by civil servants throughout the British Empire, including in Singapore and Hong Kong.[26]

Although miscegenation legislation was also never passed in Hong Kong, some related practices were in place. When architect Michael Wright joined the Crown Colony civil service, in 1938, he had to sign a form agreeing that he would not take a concubine (Wright, 2002). Up until World War Two, overseas British banks required their expatriate staff to obtain approval before they married, and everyone knew what that meant. It is said that Vandeleur Grayburn, Chief Manager of the Hong Kong and Shanghai Bank in the 1930s, looked with disfavour on most marriages to non-British women: such foreigners, natives and 'half-castes' were generally taboo (Holdsworth, 2002:195).[27] The same 'rules' applied, more or less, at what was then the Chartered Bank of India, Australia and China (now called the Standard Chartered Bank). As late as the mid-1960s, I recall, there were still cases where European employees who had married Chinese women were compelled to leave the bank.

The Commissioner of Hong Kong Police John Pennefather-Evans, appointed in 1941, apparently wanted

[26] In the 1980s and the 1990s during the run-up to the hand over of Hong Kong from Britain to China, many Chinese left Hong Kong and settled overseas. But after 1997, when people could see Hong Kong was still stable and well paid employment readily available, a number returned, in some cases leaving their families overseas.

[27] Vandeleur was tortured by the Japanese and died in a prison camp during the Second World War. He is buried in Stanley Cemetery in Hong Kong. The HongKong and Shanghai Bank later became the HongKong and Shanghai Banking Corporation. In more recent years, as it grew more global, the name changed to HSBC.

to ban inter-racial marriages between European policemen and Asian women 'because of the standard of morality typical of lower-class Asian women'. He also stressed the 'inconvenience' of Chinese spouses living in European Government quarters (Snow, 2003:201). The next Commissioner, Colonel C. H. Sansom, in the position from 1946, held similar views (Welsh, 1993:381).

As well as 'protected women', 'downhomers' or 'concubines', there were a very limited number of lawful Western-Chinese marriages in the early years of British people living in Hong Kong. Some see the World War Two period as the start of the loosening of the taboo. Among staff of the British Army Aid Group (BAAG) in southern China, attitudes were certainly more relaxed, and fraternising took place. Under wartime conditions on active service, when lives may depend on one another, it is difficult to imagine conditions being otherwise. It has also been said that the Hong Kong Volunteer Defence Corps (the Hong Kong Regiment) was one of the few organisations in which there was little racism, even in peacetime.[28]

Law in colonial Hong Kong was unusual, as is demonstrated with concubinage. When the British occupied the territory in 1841, it was agreed that Chinese laws and customs should supersede the laws and customs of England, except when a Chinese law was 'repugnant to those immutable principles of morality which Christians must regard as binding on themselves at all times and in all places ...'(Endacott, 1958:39). Concubinage was evidently not seen as 'repugnant'

[27] *I recall however attending Summer Camp as a Special Constable in the summer of 1955 when an English colleague complained that Europeans and Eurasians shared the same sleeping accommodation.*

by the British, who also did not want to be accused of not living up to their word. Looking at the history of the human race across cultures, the concept of a strictly observed monogamous matrimony is relatively new compared to polygamy which has been much more widespread, if not the norm.

In Mainland China, the Nationalists made an attempt to outlaw concubinage when they came to power in 1911, but their new laws were not properly enforced. With the Communist Revolution of 1949, women who were reminded that they 'held up half the sky' (能頂半邊天), were given a more egalitarian role in society, and in the early 1950s, the taking of concubines was no longer permitted. Singapore enacted legislation in the mid 1960s.

In the 1960s Hong Kong, there was a movement for women's rights under the leadership of Dr Ellen Li, and people like Dr Irene Cheng. They gradually gained influence and one thing they campaigned for was the abolition of concubinage (Li, 1997:VI). At one social gathering, Dr Li discussed the myths of infertility (Ingrams, 1952:111).

> 'It's all nonsense, this talk of men having to take concubines because their wives are infertile. I was reading my husband's [Dr Li Shu Pui, then director of the Hong Kong Sanatorium] British Medical Journal the other day. There was an article showing that, in the majority of cases, it is the men who are infertile, Li said. 'Most surprisingly, it was written by a man.'

It was not until 1971 that Hong Kong enacted the Marriage Reform Ordinance which banned Chinese people from taking new concubines; those already existing remained as such.

It must be said that not all Hong Kong women were in favour of doing away with concubines; some were only too happy to keep their husbands out of their own bedrooms. I also clearly remember hearing it said, in 1971: 'I'd rather the 'old man' comes home early at night to see his young concubine than staying out late when I don't know what he's up to!'

Under the old Chinese law, the traditional concubine had her rightful and recognised place within the Chinese family and society. It is not the same as a Hong Kong Chinese man keeping a mistress over the border in China, as is frequently done today. These cross-border mistresses (or a mistress in Hong Kong) have no legal protection. In the past, concubines had been built into the tax system; a Hong Kong Chinese husband could claim tax relief for supporting his secondary wives.

At a seminar on women's history held at the University of Hong Kong in May 2003, one participant argued that Britain had taken far too long to abolish concubinage in Hong Kong. After then, the children of 'mistresses' (as opposed to concubines in the past) would not be entitled to inherit property from their father. Another woman stated strongly that concubinage was not such a bad thing. This Chinese woman said that there was room for 'different kinds of marriages' in addition to the monogamous one advocated so strongly in the West. With concubinage, for example, the family remained intact and it seems that the wives and concubines usually got on reasonably well together and lived together as one family.

Some men in Hong Kong today still have concubines from before 1971, and many middle aged Chinese people will say that they have four (or whatever the number was) 'mothers'. It was suggested recently to me, partly with tongue in cheek by a Cantonese husband, that 'women only have themselves to blame' as it was they who were keen to do away with concubinage. As a mistress they have no 'protection'.

Chinese customary marriage, which had been common practice in Chinese communities around the world, was now also illegal in Hong Kong with the 1971 legislation. At such functions – where, with a Western-Chinese couple in Hong Kong, the husband was frequently a seafarer, works supervisor, jailor or policeman – a dinner was normally held at which the diners, as witnesses, duly signed on the customary 'lucky-vermilion cloth' (嘉賓提名布) as they entered the wedding banquet, usually at a restaurant (*Hong Kong 1971*, 1972). These signatures could be produced at any time as evidence of the legality of the 'marriage'. This tradition remains today in many Chinese communities around the world. After the wedding ceremony – held in a church or in registry offices – guests at the reception still sign their names on the bright red, silky cloth. It is as if they are saying, as they take the felt pen or ink brush, 'Yes, I was here. I have attended 'the red event' (紅事) [an older name for a wedding]. I believe in the love of this couple.'

marching to a different drummer

If a man does not keep pace with his companions,
perhaps it is because he hears a different drummer.
Let him march to the music he hears, however
measured or far away.

Henry David Thoreau

There have always been rebels among us, people who
do not follow the band, do not marry the girl next door, and
do not follow the status quo. People who hear a different
'drummer' and choose to do things differently. In spite of
opposition and contrasting cultures and lifestyles, some of
these have married across the racial divide.

Lulu Nathoy (her alias) is a fascinating case in point.
Originally from northern China, she was auctioned off as a
slave in San Francisco in 1870, during the days of The Wild
West (Matchett, 1981:and McCunn, 1981). An extraordinary
woman pioneer with a strong character, Lulu was taken to a
mining camp where she was the only Chinese woman. When
her owner lost her in a poker game at the camp, she was freed
by the winner. In return, Lulu later saved his life by picking
a bullet from his body with a crochet hook. They eventually
married, in spite of miscegenation laws that would extend, in

some States, all the way until 1967.

Over in England, the marriage in London in 1881, between Kai Ho Kai and Alice Walkden, '... was probably the first Anglo-Chinese (official) marriage ever', according to the late Dr Gerald Choa in *The Life and Times of Sir Kai Ho Kai*. (Choa, 1981:21). Whether this is true or not, we cannot be certain, but what is surprising is that it ever took place in racist, Victorian society. The two families must have been very liberal for their day. Ho Kai's grandfather emigrated from Guangdong to Malacca as a labourer; later, his clergyman father moved to Hong Kong, where Ho Kai was born in 1859, and educated until the early 1870s.

In Britain, Ho Kai qualified both as a medical doctor and as a lawyer. His father-in-law, John Walkden, was believed to have been a Member of Parliament at Westminister. Alice was said to have been one of the most gracious ladies ever to step into the Colony of Hong Kong. There appear to be no records as to how the couple was accepted in Hong Kong's racist and class conscious society, although the Governor, Sir John Pope Hennessy, himself married to a Eurasian[29] and a leader who occasionally took a defiant stand in supporting the Chinese, made this announcement at the Legislative Council meeting on 7th February 1882:

> 'This young gentleman [Ho Kai] who was expected to arrive in the Colony had taken the highest honours at Lincoln's Inn. It was something that a gentleman belonging to the Colony should have gained such honours' (Choa, 1981:22).

A still earlier date for a marriage between a Westerner and a Chinese in Hong Kong is sometimes cited, and papers in the Public Records Office show that Daniel Richard Caldwell and Mary Ayo W. Chan were married in St. John's Cathedral on 12 March 1851. The bride was unable to write so she made a mark (a cross). There is some doubt, however, and Caldwell could have been Eurasian. A brilliant linguist and a government servant on more than one occasion, Caldwell was a controversial figure who had interests in brothels, and was finally dismissed from the civil service.

In China, a member of the British Consular staff, J. A. T. Meadows, married a Chinese woman in the mid – nineteenth century (Coates, 1988:442). Neither the Chief Superintendent Minister nor the Foreign Minister displayed unease about his marriage, even though the wife was illiterate, and the union could have been viewed as 'marrying down'. Yet, his marriage did not bar him later from becoming a respected and successful merchant in the largely British city of Tientsin.

Other cases in China, this time involving Chinese men and Western women, often teenagers, were revealed in a Shanghai newspaper in 1898 (Macartney, 1898:520). According to Sir Halliday Macartney, Secretary to the Chinese Legation in London at the time, some of the Chinese husbands were honourable, well-educated and of good social standing in China, and included Chinese officials in the Legation in London. Their brides were generally not of the same standing in Britain.

At around the same time, as reported in the same newspaper article, there were also said to be four young English women (possibly more) married to Chinese seamen who were brought back to Shanghai by mail steamer. Not all these marriages seemed to be working well. One young bride was reported to have been friendless, penniless, wearing nothing but a nightdress in an empty house, where she was heard by a neighbour crying for twelve hours.

About a decade later, W. J. B. Fletcher, a second assistant in the British Consular Corps working in the city of Hoihow (Haikou) on Hainan Island, married a woman named Tsoi Yan Siu who lived in Hong Kong. When he was granted home leave, in 1908, it became known that he sailed for Hong Kong, and that he visited his wife there, a literate woman from a respected but impoverished family (Coates, 1988:442). When questioned in an enquiry, he stated that life suited him among the Chinese, whom he liked, and that he had lost touch with Britain. The authorities said Fletcher had 'lost caste' and put forward the case that 'lonely and remote' postings around the world often put temptation in the way of officers. The authorities claimed that Fletcher would now be seen as an equal to his wife's relatives and friends, many or all of whom held menial jobs. In many ways, the Fletchers were unfortunate. Had they married fifty years earlier, as Meadows did, they would not have encountered major difficulties. In the same way, had they married in the second half of the twentieth century, there would have been no significant problem.

To make matters worse, Fletcher was later involved in a case in which a Chinese girl was kidnapped and later murdered aboard a ship; in the end it was seen by the authorities that his interracial marriage had rendered him unsuitable to hold a senior post in the service. He was pensioned off. Fletcher remained in China, became a professor of English at Sun Yat Sen University in Guangzhou, and died in 1933. In 1920, after more information came to light, his name was cleared, and it was concluded Fletcher had 'rendered signal service to justice'. Fletcher and his wife are buried in the Hong Kong Cemetery in Happy Valley where, on their gravestone, Fay Fletcher is described as William Fletcher's 'beloved wife'.

Charlie Coalbrook is one of the few pre-World War Two European soldiers to marry, and to stay with his Chinese girlfriend. They wed in St. Andrew's Church, in Kowloon, Hong Kong, in 1939. When asked if he was discriminated against because of his marriage, he replied, 'Well yes. I suffered slightly. It certainly cost me a rank, but when they found out Violet's uncle was a director of the Sincere Department Store, that made a difference' (Wolfendale, mid-1990s:23). The devoted couple settled in England, and made an annual pilgrimage back to Hong Kong's wartime sites until Violet's death in the 1990s.

During World War Two, as indicated in the last chapter, more and more intermarriages occurred in Hong Kong, particularly between Westerners and Eurasians: W. P. (Tommy) Thompson of the Hong Kong Police married

Eurasian Irene Fincher (nee Gittens) (Snow, 2003:402), and Major Ronald Holmes, a Hong Kong Government Administrative Officer who acted as Colonial Secretary after the war, married the Eurasian Marjorie Fisher (Hall, 1992:80,138-9). **30**

Arthur Bentley was one of the first high-profile members of the community, as the Hong Kong Government Pharmacist, to marry a Hong Kong Chinese woman. His wife, Leung Man-wah, taught at universities in China and Hong Kong, and went to Oxford University as a Rhodes scholar in 1944. Leung says she was one of the first University of Hong Kong woman graduates to marry a European.

Many other well-known personalities, in various walks of life, were also not afraid to 'march to a different drummer' and enter into an interracial marriage with their loved one. Here are just a few of these couples, presented chronologically.

K.M.A. (Ken) and Joan Barnett, married in the 1940s

Ken Barnett, a jovial Englishman, joined the Colonial Service and was posted to Hong Kong as a young cadet officer in 1932. A Lieutenant, he commanded the 4th Battery, Corps of Artillery, in the Hong Kong Volunteer Defence Corps during the attack by Japanese soldiers in December 1941. **31** Barnett was said to have been the first person to spot the first wave of Japanese as they came at night across Lei Yue Mun Straits to attack Hong Kong Island. When he reported this to his commanding officer, he was told to pull himself together:

30 On occasions, views have been expressed that Ronald Holmes was denied promotion to the most senior posts in the colonial service because of his marriage to a Eurasian. (Snow,2003:323)(Hall,1992:138). There appears to be no solid evidence to support this.

31 Right up until the early 1960s, every able bodied British Subject had to serve part-time, in the Hong Kong Regiment (The Volunteers), as a Special Constable or in Essential Services.

'You're imagining things, Barnett.'

A fellow prisoner, Dr Solomon Bard, tells how in prison camp K.M.A. Barnett spoke up to the visiting Swiss Red Cross officials about a shortage of food and medicine; for his act of great courage, he was badly beaten by his captors (Bard, 1987:8). Barnett's girlfriend at the time, a Fujianese Chinese who took the Western name of Joan, also ran the risk of being beaten or stripped naked, when she brought him food at the camp, putting it through the wire fence. The two married shortly after the war, and, from all appearances, their union was a happy one.

Ken could speak Cantonese, and two or three other Chinese dialects. Barnett wrote and published a number of erudite papers about sinology, and some colleagues respected his linguistic abilities and his knowledge of 'Things Chinese'.[32] Others, my old boss for one, criticised Barnett for going 'overboard'. Sir Samuel Bonham, Governor of Hong Kong from 1848 to 1854, once said that the study of Chinese addled the brain (Spurr, 1995:40). I too remember hearing similar remarks around the time of my marriage in 1960. When studying Greek and Latin was considered a good mental exercise to 'sharpen' the brain, some of us found it hard to see how studying Chinese would 'addle' it.

Although Barnett was a District Commissioner for the New Territories, the late journalist Derek Davies wrote that perhaps it was Barnett's marriage that had blocked his promotion to the highest echelons of Government, although there was no explicit policy on this issue after World War Two,

The articles are published in the Journal of the Hong Kong Branch of the Royal Asiatic Society.

[33]

and no prohibition in the Terms of Service (Davies, 1987:5). It could be that some promotion boards genuinely felt, in spite of Barnett having a brilliant mind, that he had shortcomings in certain areas. I know there were people who felt he was so mesmerised by Chinese culture (he was even able to compose Chinese poetry), that he was unlikely to be able to take a balanced and objective view involving British interests. Davies, however, added that he instinctively found it comforting when those wielding power spent their spare hours writing poetry (Davies, 1987:7).

It is loyalty, however, which is inherently valued within any civil service, or by any organisation. This is evident with the 'security checks' that are carried out on recruitment to any government or on promotion to senior positions. In our survey, the security rating of one ex-soldier in the British armed forces was downgraded when he married a Chinese.

The opinions of the wives of senior British officers also seemed to carry a certain amount of weight, with such comments as, 'After all, no 'nice' person would marry outside his or her race.' When Barnett visited the Flower Market at the Lunar New Year wearing a *cheung min po* (長棉袍) [a long, padded, Chinese gown], there were a few sniggers among these wives and the hint that the poor chap had 'gone native'.

After his thirty-seven years with the Colonial Service, Ken Barnett (Hayes, 1987:1) retired not caring too much what anyone thought of him or his private life. Ken, Joan and their daughter Ruby lived for a short time in Malawi, which rt="

was formerly a British protectorate, before settling for good in England.

Anonymous British Royal Navy Seaman and his Mainland Chinese wife, probably married in the 1950s or 1960s

One British able seaman who served on a Royal Navy ship anchored in Hong Kong harbour received a certain amount of publicity in the early 1950s. He was well known among his mates as having strong communist leanings and, to get to the point, he jumped ship. No one really seemed to know how, but he managed to get over the border into the People's Republic of China. Living there, he studied the language, married a Chinese woman probably in the late 1950s, had a family and became an official interpreter for the People's Republic of China. Little is known about the man as, in those days, although there were 'China Watchers' stationed in Hong Kong, who spent much of their time questioning refugees, information was not easy to obtain.

He, of course, lived through events like the 'Great Leap Forward' (1959-1960), when the economy was badly managed and agriculture was neglected, resulting in the starvation of about thirty million people in the early 1960s.[33] The Great Proletarian Cultural Revolution followed, from 1966 to 1976, when the population turned against its own culture. The cry went up, 'Condemn the Four Olds' (除四舊) [old customs, old habits, old culture and old thoughts]! To

[33] There used to be long queues at the time in the post offices in Hong Kong with residents sending food parcels to relatives and friends in China.

what extent was this ex-naval officer involved and how have these events affected his life? Was he persecuted?

After the Open Door Policy commenced, in December 1978, he travelled to the West on at least one occasion as a translator with an official People's Republic of China party. When he passed through Hong Kong on his way back to the Mainland, newspapers reported his arrival.

I have often wondered about him. Is he still alive? Has he any regrets? He is most likely the only Western spouse in this book who has adopted a totally Mainland Chinese lifestyle, and in such an official government capacity.

Alan Pickford and Ho Lai Sheung, married in 1952

Not too long after the Second World War ended, Alan Pickford, a twenty-year old British corporal in the Royal Army Pay Corps, was stationed in Hong Kong (Parry, 2002:6). The Colony was a very exciting place for a young soldier. He started learning Cantonese, which was unusual for servicemen at the time, and it all began at a ballroom dancing class when he met Ho Lai Sheung, from Canton (as it was called then). She spoke no English.

'She looked super!' were his exact words. It was not long before he asked her to spend the rest of her life with him. He could see there were three main obstacles: the Methodist Church, the family, and the army. Someone at the Church said, 'You don't want to marry one of those "little yellow monkeys" surely?' I told them, 'Christianity knows no bounds.' Alan wrote to his father who replied, 'East is East and West is West.' I wrote back and said things had changed a bit since Kipling's day. The 'battle' went on for about six months. One Friday, he requested permission from the army to marry, and on the following Monday, he was promptly posted to Singapore. Pickford insists, 'I believe I wore them down.'

Eventually, Ho Lai Sheung took a ship to Singapore where they were married at a registry office. This caused a sensation in Britain. *The Sunday Times* took up the story of how a British corporal had met a beautiful 'Goddess of the Moon', and that it had taken three months for Pickford to learn to say *Ngor oi nei* (我愛你) [I love you] in Cantonese (Parry, 2002:6). Another newspaper laid on a champagne dinner at the Cafe Royal in Manchester, 'but we never did get to drink the champagne,' Pickford said. 'It was for show.'

Visiting Hong Kong in December 2002, ahead of their golden wedding anniversary, Lai Sheung said, 'I have never regretted marrying Alan for one moment.' The couple had overcome the racial and social divide. There was talk of their story being made into a film at one stage (Parry, 2002:6).

Helmut Sohmen and Pao Pei-qing (Anna Sohmen), married in the 1960s

Before World War Two, only the lower ranks of European society, with a few exceptions, would occasionally engage in Western-Chinese marriages. That was not the case after the War, and a good example is the Austrian Helmut Sohmen, who married the eldest daughter of the Pao family.

Sir Y. K. Pao (1918-1991) came to Hong Kong from Shanghai in the mid-1940s and quickly built up a fleet of ships larger than that of Stavros Niarchos and Aristotle Onassis (Hong Kong Standard, 1989:17). Very much an international personality, the shipping magnate was acquainted with British prime ministers, U.S. President Ronald Regan, the late Deng Xiaoping, and many other world leaders besides.

His eldest daughter was Pao Pei-qing. Pei means 'accompanying' and Qing means 'celebrated, happy tidings', as she was born in Chongqing, the 'accompanying' capital of China. (During World War Two, Nanjing was occupied by the Japanese, therefore the Chinese set up their capital in Chongqing.) Her Western name was Anna. Sir Y. K. would have a total of four daughters, Anna, Bessie, Cissy and Doreen, A B C and D, in descending order by age. A systematic man, Sir Y. K. always used to say, 'It's easier to remember the girls like that. It's a little like naming ships.' Anna's younger sisters married a Shanghainese, a Japanese, and the youngest married a Cantonese, but has since become divorced.

While studying in Canada, Anna met the young Helmut, who was working in Montreal as a lawyer. His first visit to Hong Kong was in December of 1967, the Year of the Riots. (Sohmen, 2004:88) Although by the end of that year the situation was beginning to change, it had been a bad time for Hong Kong, with considerable industrial unrest coupled with violent demonstrations against British colonial rule. Bombs were even planted. Although the bulk of the population had no choice but to sit it out, a number of citizens left the Colony or made preparations to do so. Sohmen wrote, 'Optimists were in short supply' (2004:89).

Eventually father-in-law managed to persuade Helmut to work in the Pao family enterprise of World-Wide Shipping (Sohmen, 2004:89). Helmut and Anna arrived in Hong Kong in 1970, after he had spent some time in their hectic London Office '... with our Canadian daughter and five suitcases.' Helmut said that, as an Austrian-Chinese couple, they were cordially received by the small Austrian community in Hong Kong as well as by the Pao family.

He relates that he had not reckoned on what was the verbal equivalent of the 'Chinese water torture' at the time, by father-in-law, to persuade him to come to Hong Kong to live. The family shipping business was expanding rapidly, and with a twelve-hour working day, a wife teaching at the University of Hong Kong and a new son (who later became Head Boy at Eton College in England), there was little time for anything else. Anna's major interests have been in sociology and child psychology, but she and her husband became active with the newly established Hong Kong Academy of the Performing Arts, with Helmut acting as Chairman. He was also a Legislative Councilor in Colonial Hong Kong during the 1980s and 1990s.

[34] *There has been talk of the need to set up a museum in Hong Kong in memory of Bruce Lee but, at the time of writing, it has yet to materialise.*

[35] *I had a colleague whose real name in Chinese was 'Ox'. His parents believed by naming him after an animal of limited value, evil influences would desist from carrying their son away. Later, he was embarrassed by the name and went through the legal process of changing it.*

Bruce Lee and Linda Emery, married in 1964

Martial arts legend Bruce Lee (1940-1973) is usually claimed to be one of Hong Kong's most famous sons (Block, 1974).[34] Actually, he was born in San Francisco in 1940, but a few months after his birth, the family moved to Kowloon, Hong Kong, where he lived until 1959. He left after a fight that led to trouble with the Hong Kong Police, and being a citizen of the United States, he took a steamboat back to San Francisco with US$100 in his pocket. His Chinese name after all was Jun Fan (振藩), meaning 'return again', as his mother Grace felt that he would indeed return to live in the States again.

At home, Lee was usually called Sai Fan, meaning 'Little San Francisco', the city where he was born. He was also sometimes called 'Little Phoenix' by his family, even though he was born in the Year of the Dragon and in the hour of the Dragon. 'Dragon' connotes a strong male, which an evil spirit might be tempted to steal, a fear for many Chinese parents. Therefore, he was called 'Phoenix' to suggest a weaker female, thus tricking the spirits to believe the child was relatively worthless.[35]

Many Chinese people like to think of Bruce as being totally Chinese. Yet while his father was Chinese, the Cantonese opera star Lee Hoi Chuen, his mother was a Roman Catholic Eurasian. Bruce Lee also had a white, American wife named Linda, who with her blonde hair, has often been characterised as being an 'all American girl'. It was Chinese martial arts that brought the two together – she was a student in his first Gung Fu (Kung Fu) institute in Seattle, her hometown. In fact, teaching martial arts to non-Asians was not accepted by some members of the Chinese community there.

Linda's family did not approve of her wanting to marry a Chinese man. When news got out about them applying for a marriage license, her extended family held an all-day meeting to try to dissuade Linda from the marriage. Linda wrote in her biography of Bruce Lee that, 'my aunt and uncle were very religious and they thought the mixing of the races was abomination' (Lee, 1989:19). Still, the objections only seemed to strengthen the couple's resolve, and they married in August, 1964. The following year, soon after their son Brandon was born, Bruce introduced his wife and infant boy to his family in Hong Kong. They stayed with the Lee family in Kowloon for four months. Bruce's family would have preferred him to marry a Chinese woman, but in her autobiography Linda said she 'did not receive any of the prejudicial reaction Bruce had endured with my family.'

Elsie Hume and Andrew Tu, met in the 1950s

Elsie Hume, born in 1913 in Newcastle-upon-Tyne in the north of England, went to China with her first husband, Bill Elliott, before the People's Republic of China was established in 1949. They worked as missionaries. But life became difficult under the Communists, and the couple moved to Hong Kong, where she, Mrs Elliott, set up the Mu Kuang English School for poor Chinese children in Kowloon City, and also championed the underprivileged. She was passionate about many public causes, and was always ready to take on the British Colonial Government although she was accused, in earlier years especially, of frequently not taking a balanced view and being too subjective. She sat as a member of the Urban Council and the Legislative Council, and was much later made a Commander of the British Empire.

In her book, *Shouting at the Mountain*, published in 2004, after her second husband Andrew died, Elsie says that, often on a Friday evening in the 1960s Andrew Tu, then her long-time companion, would take her out for dinner and perhaps to the cinema. But, as she said, 'His world understood mine almost as little as mine understood his.' (Tu, 2004:191). She went on to say that a European woman walking beside a Chinese man aroused suspicions in those days that 'he was a hanger-on using the woman for his advancement.'

Quite late in life, Elsie married her long-time companion, Andrew Tu who was born into a poor family in Inner Mongolia and who fled the civil war in China and came to Hong Kong. Their love ripened into a lifelong partnership (Tu, 2004). Rita Fan, Chairperson of the Legislative Council wrote in a circular published in the *South China Morning Post*:

> *The greatest blessing in life is to have someone by your side, holding your hand through wind and storm, sharing your joy and sorrow, and heading*

*for the same direction. For Elsie, that person was
Andrew.* (Tu, 2004)

Elsie Tu also has a strong supporter in Elsie Leung,
Secretary for Justice, who wrote:

> *No one can match Elsie Tu in her courage to
> strive for justice and total selflessness in the service
> of the Hong Kong people. In Elsie's lustrous
> political career, we can see the tower of strength
> behind her, the late Andrew Tu, who quietly gave
> her support through the stormy years. They have
> my greatest admiration* (Tu, 2004).

Jack Edwards and Tam So-lam, met in the 1970s and married in 1990

No one has done more for British, Commonwealth
and Chinese ex-servicemen, and indeed for servicemen of
many nationalities, than the stalwart Jack Edwards. Among
ex-servicemen, he is an icon, his name saluted around the world.

He served in the Royal Corps of Signals in the army in
World War Two, was captured by the Japanese after Singapore
fell, and spent the remainder of the war as a prisoner. After
hostilities ceased, he continued serving for a further three years
at war crime trials (Edwards, undated: cover). Starting in the
early 1960s, he worked in estate management in Hong Kong,
at the same time undertaking voluntary service for the Royal
British Legion as well as for prisoner-of-war associations. The
Commonwealth Veterans' Memorial on Constitution Hill in

London, unveiled by the Queen in 2000 to commemorate the five million servicemen from the Commonwealth who served with Britain in World War Two, would not have included Hong Kong on the list of territories if it had not been for Jack. He raised the question of the 'missing territory' with the Duke of Edinburgh. It was later again raised at a meeting in London where it was carried unanimously.

Tam So-lam, now Mrs Polly Edwards, ran away from home in Wuhan in Hubei Province in China, in 1949, at the age of fourteen to enlist in Chairman Mao's army (Maher, 2003). With the tumultuous years in China that followed, she was never to see her immediate family members again although she searched for them more than once. After a period in the army spent in drills, working in the fields, and attending school, she was selected to become a member of a dance troupe to entertain the Chinese troops. In 1958, she 'married' an army instructor in a 'union of mutual consent' and became pregnant four years later. Tired of waiting for her first husband to send for her from Hong Kong, where he had gone several months earlier in search of work, she burned all traces of her identity and sneaked over the border, in 1962. She never found her first husband. She credits Mao's army for making her tough enough to survive her early years in Hong Kong, where she taught Putonghua, gave birth to a daughter, learned Cantonese by day and English at night school.

Polly and Jack met at a social function. The marriage has not been without its trials, according to Jack. Perhaps the biggest hurdle was the wedding itself: the couple married in 1990, sixteen years after that first encounter (Maher, 2003:1). For many years, Polly had seen no need to marry, often saying, 'We are already happy!' Jack meanwhile really wanted her to 'carry the Edwards' name and [my] ring on her finger. 'I had difficulty in making her see how important it was for me.'

As a Welshman, Jack likes singing, and Polly likes dancing – she at one time was a dance instructor. They get along well together, and by many accounts have had a good relationship, before and after the wedding. He has been ill in recent years, and she has nursed him tenderly. Publicly, they attend Royal British Legion functions together, as well as Armistice Day Remembrance Services, and so on.

~ ~ ~

At the time of such courtships and marriages, up to the 1970s, if a Western-Chinese couple walked along the streets of Hong Kong, obscene remarks might sometimes still be made, or at least looks of discontent and discomfort, or long stares of curiosity. Nowadays, and over the past decade or so, Chinese women in Hong Kong and Mainland China report that few people bother giving a second glance. Most cross-cultural couples in this book insist they are, by and large, accepted by their communities. Of the 81 couples in this study, about half said they had never been victims of discrimination.

According to H. J. Lethbridge, a professor of sociology at the University of Hong Kong in the 1970s, there were 47 mixed marriages in Hong Kong in 1947, and 112 in 1962 (Lethbridge, 1968:128). This may not be an accurate figure since Lethbridge may have assumed that a person listed with a European name was a full-blooded European (when in fact he or she could have been Eurasian, or of other mixed heritage) and that a person with a Chinese name was 100 per cent Chinese, possibly a Eurasian, or perhaps a divorced European woman previously married to a Chinese. The general custom in most countries appears to be not to include the race or nationality of the bride or groom on a marriage certificate. This lack of information restricts research (Immigration Department, Hong Kong, 2003).

In another study, this time conducted in the United States, a greater proportion of Chinese women than Chinese men were found to have married whites. Morrison G. Wong, from Texas Christian University, came to the conclusion that 64 per cent of Western-Chinese marriages in the United States involved Chinese women (Wong, 1989: 94). In our study, this figure is greater: out of the total of 81 married couples who were surveyed or interviewed, 82 per cent consisted of Chinese women. Although by no means firm evidence, these two sets of figures seem to match the everyday reality in Hong Kong: one meets more couples where the husband is a Westerner and the wife Chinese, than the other way round. Why is this?

Generally, in communities like Singapore and Hong Kong at least, there has been a history of larger numbers of Western men than Western women among residents. Under these circumstances, the men start to look around for local, that is to say Asian, partners.

An interesting difference arises here between Western and Chinese men. Whereas Westerners were generally confident enough to approach Chinese women, the reverse does not have seemed to have been the case. Middle-aged or elderly Chinese men questioned about this have frequently agreed that, when they were young, they would have lacked confidence and been too conservative to try to date a Western woman. It is not surprising that most of the Chinese men in our survey first met their wife-to-be in the West and did much of their courting there, too.

As the men themselves pointed out, Chinese culture can be very conservative. Some Western women may not choose to marry into Chinese culture partly because of male-dominant customs. Some of these customs stem from Confucianism. Custom has it that a girl is expected to honour her father, the wife to obey her husband, and the widow to follow her eldest son.

Another reason, physiological but also psycho-social, may be that a Western woman, particularly with northern European roots, may often be taller than the average Chinese man, especially men from the southern regions of China, who tend to be smaller. A woman often likes to look up to her man whereas overly tall women may not be popular.

Returning to the research by Morrison Wong, he further predicted that the more closely the lifestyles of Westerners and Chinese resemble each other, the more English the Chinese people speak, and the greater the degree of acculturation, the greater will be the prevalence of Caucasian-Chinese marriages (Wong, 1989:87). Lethbridge had also predicted, twenty-one years earlier, that the number of mixed marriages would go on increasing. Although no conclusive research exists to support or refute these claims, the spouses taking part in our survey would likely agree with Wong and Lethridge: many expressed the view that cross-cultural marriages were becoming more frequent.

Several social forces are at play in this presumed increase. For one, there has been a marked decline in the old, racist idea of white supremacy since World War Two. To a considerable extent, in Asia at least, this was brought about by the Japanese military being able to capture places like Malaya, Singapore and Hong Kong, all of which were defended by British troops in the Second World War. This is not however the place to discuss this.

Chinese culture, and other Asian cultures, too, has become popular. There is greater interest in, and appreciation for Chinese civilisation, including cuisine, the arts, martial arts, feng shui and herbal medicine.

The strong economies of Hong Kong and Singapore, and the growth of China proper since the Open Door Policy of 1978, has drawn many more Westerners to the Far East. The standard of living has also improved, making the environment more liveable for the average Westerner, as this Western wife in the survey writes:

Things have changed very much in Hong Kong

since I first came here with my Chinese husband in 1963. I had to contend with a serious water shortage with water on tap only for four hours once every four days. I wasn't used to the heat with little air-conditioning as we have now. There were few good Western restaurants here then and no supermarkets. The worst thing for me was there was no 'Life Bread!' [insignificant things are important to some people]

The social distance between Westerners and Chinese has narrowed, as this spouse wrote in the questionnaire:

With globalisation and changing social attitudes the number of cross-cultural marriages is obviously going to increase. This phenomenon should be understood and managed and not fought against. With time, and with changing social attitudes coming more into effect, in spite of resistance from some quarters, different nations will become more alike.

Within Mainland China, the growing interest in marrying a non-Chinese is such that books have been written, even in Chinese advising people how to go about looking for a Western spouse (Lacroix, 2003). Among the best places to look, these books indicate, are bars, hotels and the work place. The how-to books list a number of questions to ask such as, 'Tell me a joke in English to see if I laugh.'

A marriage counsellor, who is in daily contact with mixed marriage couples in Hong Kong, agrees that cross-cultural marriages are becoming more common and more readily accepted. On average, she says that three out of every ten clients at her centre are in a cross-cultural marriage; these include Chinese married to Indians, to Filipinos and to Europeans. She says that while Chinese see Westerners as being more open and less conservative, her experience is that many of her Chinese clients are in fact very open, not at all conservative, and spouses are very patient with expatriate spouses. Another marriage counselling centre aims to counsel couples before they marry. The two partners pro-actively state what they expect from the relationship and the ensuing discussions are guided professionally.

Lethbridge postulated that most inter-racial marriages take place only after a period of serious deliberation (Lethbridge, 1968:128). He goes on to say that in most of these marriages, emotional bonds are strong, and that partners work hard to make their marriage a success. He also hypothesises that inter-racial marriages are more durable than same culture marriages. These seem to be sweeping statements, and I am aware of no figures or evidence to support them, yet the findings of this study do seem to correspond, to some degree. Among the 81 couples in the survey, there were only two cases of divorce, and only two couples who stated that their marriages were not happy.

Some couples in our study insisted that Western-Chinese marriages are basically no different from same-culture marriages and the difficulties are no greater: 'although we look different, we are the same.' Other spouses are more cautious, believing that two sometimes antagonistic cultures can add a difficult dimension into the equation, and that more effort is required. One spouse contributes this view:

> *My husband and I think it is important to respect*
> *that people have different ways of doing things.*
> *This is especially true for cross-cultural marriages.*
> *Problems may develop when both partners do*
> *not define clearly the source of misunderstanding.*
> *'Cultural differences' must not be used as an excuse*
> *for inadequate communication of feelings.*

With the old Chinese system of arranged marriages, the Chinese attempted to avoid the predictable problems arising from the pairing of two dissimilar partners. In those days, in Imperial China, it was often the wife who was expected to compromise; today, both partners are expected to find ways to accommodate each other.

A useful and more modern model to categorise inter-racial marriages is Dugan Romano's Types of Intercultural Marriages: Submission / Immersion, Obliteration, Compromise, and Consensus (Romano, 2001:171).

There are couples in our study where one spouse has immersed him or herself almost entirely in their spouse's lifestyle, largely abandoning her or his own culture, or at least keeping it in the background. Submission / Immersion is more frequently found among older couples where the wife is not well educated; it is more common among women than men, and more common among Chinese men than Western men. There are Chinese wives in our study who live with white husbands in Europe or North America who seemingly adopted an almost entirely Western lifestyle. This may not be totally by choice. In the West, she or he may have limited contact with the family and the culture.

There are also couples in our survey, living in places like Singapore and Hong Kong, who frequently follow largely western lifestyles because the European husband is not comfortable with Chinese ways, and he probably speaks little if any Chinese. Romano says that many people believe Submission / Immersion can be the most functional model in that, if both spouses are able to accept it, it reduces the risks of conflict and gives a clearer sense of identity to the children with well defined roots in one culture. A Chinese wife moving to Europe or elsewhere to live may find she cannot entirely wipe out her many years of upbringing and erase the inner core of her being. With love for her own country and culture still intact, she may find herself having to do things in her adopted land with which she does not entirely agree. She may miss chatting in her own language at the street market, and knowing that body language, too. How do they express themselves? Is there much arm waving? She may miss being respected for who she really, fully, is. She may have a longing to eat succulent chicken feet which no one else in the family can bear. One Chinese wife who has 'immersed' herself in her husband's culture said she has devoted herself to their children and him, 'My job is to keep the family happy.' While this attitude may be very noble, it can also be martyr-like, and she may wreck her own happiness along the way, and eventually upset her marriage.

In the second method, Obliteration (Romano, 2001:173), couples try to cope with isolated differences by blotting them out. One or both spouses may be called upon, largely or partially, to give up their own language, and part of their native culture and lifestyle. When people emigrate, they may do their best to identify with their adopted country. In our survey, a Continental European woman married a Chinese man and they settled in a third country, England. They themselves resisted, as far as this was possible, adopting the local lifestyle. The children were not brought up with any British ways, and in some respects, they lacked support. The whole family tended to be 'culture poor', although both partners told their children tales about when they themselves were young in their home countries. It could well be that the Eurasian children love England and identify with it. The country is 'home' and they get on well at school, particularly with sports and games, and they are capable of standing up for themselves.

Many of the couples in our study adopt Compromise, the third approach, without perhaps fully realising it. Here, both spouses give up certain aspects of their culturally bound beliefs and adopt some of the beliefs of their partner (Romano 2001:174). It amounts to incorporating a series of 'trade offs'. For example, 'We will continue to send money to support your ageing parents (which I am not happy about) in China, but, we agree we will retire in Canada.' Such open and flexible compromising can be viewed as gaining and losing, giving and taking, and is an arrangement entered into by both parties with good intentions. To illustrate this among couples in our survey, there are a small number of Europeans who do not enjoy eating Chinese food, and whose Chinese spouses are not fond of Western dishes. Although it means extra work, this is sometimes overcome by eating different meals: 'one family, two kitchens.' Another example in our survey is a couple which in the past had attended church together. When the wife lost her faith, the husband, albeit reluctantly, accepted that he had now to go alone. If a couple arrives at a number of compromises, they may reach consensus, which is the next arrangement.

Consensus depends again on give-and-take (Romano, 2001:175). A more refined and advanced form of Compromise, it requires both partners to feel secure enough to allow their spouse, to a degree, to do their own thing, 'to be different'. This is not to be considered a form of 'betrayal' or taken as a threat by the other spouse. Things are either worked out harmoniously, or they fall into place naturally, without either partner 'losing face'. In our survey, a few Chinese wives usually meet their Chinese friends on their own, as their husbands do not feel comfortable in their company possibly because of lack of language skills or due to different food preferences. Such a compromise, in the form of a consensus, allows spouses to keep in touch with their roots and to look both inside and outside their marriage for ways to achieve a happy life.

What would the participants of this study say are the important ingredients of a successful Western-Chinese marriage? The following list, which differs from Romano's compilation (Romano, 2001:183), is not exhaustive, nor are the items necessarily listed in order of importance.

1   A spirit of adventure and a ready acceptance of customs which are different.

2   Confidence in oneself and a positive self image.

3   Love as a major motivating force.

4   A strong commitment to the marriage.

5   Sensitivity towards each other in spite of cultural differences.

6   A need to be able to communicate and an ability to avoid misunderstandings.

7   Flexible goals and adaptability to a changing lifestyle.

8   An interest in the spouse's culture and customs.

9   Ability to get along with the spouse's relatives and friends.

10   A sense of humour.

One European wife and her Chinese husband in our survey offered the following advice, no doubt with the best of intentions:

> Be realistic in choosing where to live and anticipating what problems might occur. If there are great cultural differences, give your partner a slow, interactive course on important social skills he or she will need in order not to offend anybody. If one

partner is unwilling to compromise or change, don't
get married.

~ ~ ~

Let us take a look at two cases of Western-Chinese couples which developed problems at stages in their marriage.

Case Study One: A Briton living in Hong Kong came into a marriage counselling centre alone, in the early 1960s. His Chinese wife had run away, and he wanted someone to find her. The counsellor explained that was not her job and, in any case, she did not have the resources to do so. The husband explained that although he often told his wife he loved her and wanted to hold her hand, she never responded. He complained that he loved his Chinese wife much more than she loved him. He appreciated that even if a person is fluent in a language, they may have difficulty in expressing feelings or defining things like love.

Time passed, and the Englishman came in again to see the counsellor, this time with his wife. They were living together again. In some ways, they were a fairly typical Western-Chinese, or even 'same-culture' Chinese, couple: he was older, better educated, and held a more senior position, and she had been a secretary in his firm and was now a full-time housewife with a maid to assist with caring for their two lovely daughters.

The husband again told the counsellor that he loved his wife far more than she loved him. The wife denied this, and confirmed she loved her husband very much. It is not so common for Chinese to display their affection, she said, complaining that her husband was always abrupt and did not listen. 'You say I do not love you,' she said. 'Have you not noticed! I cook a new dish for you every night! Is there a better way to show my love? The quickest way to a man's heart should be through his stomach!'

She admitted, in the Chinese way, much of her time was spent looking after their two daughters rather than pampering her husband. She said she hoped he would understand. They both agreed eventually that many of their problems had been caused by misunderstandings, and that their different cultures have different ways of defining gender roles.

Some years later, the marriage counsellor heard that the husband had retired and the family had gone to England to live, as they wanted their Eurasian daughters to be brought up in an English environment. The family came back occasionally on visits to Hong Kong, and they all seemed to be getting on well together.

Case Study Two: A couple, a Chinese man with his better educated German wife, went to see a marriage counsellor for help. The husband, who had a hard upbringing and by habit counted every cent, had purchased some furniture and thought he had obtained a real bargain. His German wife did not like the furniture at all, and told him so in her direct, take-it-or-leave-it way, 'You lack taste!' He chided her, and pointed out that Chinese people would communicate such opinions in indirect ways. 'We Chinese really know how to give people face.'

Another recent disagreement had revolved around language. She felt it was important for their children to learn German, as they might have to return to Germany one day. The Chinese husband, who had completed only ten years of schooling, found it a difficult language to learn, and he felt like an outsider when his wife and children spoke fluent German with one another. Children and mothers often tend to have a 'mother-tongue alliance', which the husband, in this case, had difficulty in accepting. The husband insisted it was too much for the children to learn three languages – English, Cantonese and German – and he wanted the children to drop the German. In fact, they seemed to be handling the three languages very well; the truth was that he himself could not meet the challenge.

Traditionally, Chinese feel it is better that a women 'marries up': that her husband is better qualified, and he older than herself. A husband, meanwhile should 'marry down'. Some Chinese women are often loath to marry beneath themselves, feeling it is more shameful than staying single. 'We can live comfortably without men [some career women say]... we don't want [them] to share our wealth, or even worse, to drain our wealth and resources.' (Wang, 2004).

The counsellor lost touch with the couple shortly afterwards.

~ ~ ~

Some couples go to their religious leader, a priest or

rabbi, in times of need. In this case, it was the mother of a Chinese woman who married a Westerner. In a newsletter item, 'Did God want Chinese and Europeans to intermarry?' published by Saint Joseph's Roman Catholic Church in Hong Kong, a parishioner was quoted:

> *Dear Father,*
>
> *My daughter, who is working on her doctoral degree, recently married a European. I just cannot accept this. I may be wrong, but I don't think God meant for Europeans and Chinese to marry. I cannot even go to Mass without feeling like I've done something wrong in bringing up my daughter* (St Joseph's Church: c.1997).
>
> (signed) *'Feeling Bad'*

Paraphrased below is the Parish Priest's reply:

Dear 'Feeling Bad',

Although society has come a long way, interracial marriage is still a tough issue for some people no matter the race. This is particularly true when a mixed marriage takes place in 'our' family. We become irrational and cannot think clearly. One big problem is prejudice, a prejudgment that one race is better than another. Why did your daughter marry a man who happens to be another colour? Presumably because she loves him. We live in a rainbow-coloured [multi-racial] *world where, in theory, many different colours are equally beautiful. There is nothing in God's law or the law of the Church that prevents a person from marrying someone of another race.*

I do not mean it is not a crisis in your life. It is probably equally difficult for the parents of your daughter's husband. Your daughter will have some worrying days ahead and will need your support more than ever. Society will cause enough harm and pain for your daughter and her husband. There will be stares, frowns and scowls. These will cause enough trouble without having to face more from those closest to them.

The reply was signed, 'Your Pastor.'

In a similar vein to 'Feeling Bad', columnist Rebecca Woo wrote in *Asia Magazine* (now defunct, but which used to have a wide circulation on Sundays in the Far East) that inter-racial marriages go against social norms and only result in unhappiness. She wrote:

Why should 'half-ghost' children, 'symbols of disgrace', have to bear the brunt of their parents' selfish selection of a marriage partner by breaking homogeneity of race? [36] *We live in a practical world. Life is easier if we face up to reality* (Woo, 1986: 'My Word' column).

In subsequent weeks, replies came in to Asia Magazine thick and fast. The late Bill Lowe, writer and teacher, dismissed

[36] *Because Europeans looked so pale, Chinese called them 'ghost' people at first sighting. The name has stuck.*

her attitude as that of a socio-racial bigot, a 'closed-minded Victorian or Confucian dyed-in-the-wool dogmatist'. The Londoner said his response was based on his twenty years of 'hilariously happy marriage' ('That Racial Mix', 1986:11).

Here are other excerpts from replies to Woo:

- Children are colour blind. They are racially indifferent.
- Most children of mixed marriages are uniquely beautiful.

One reader called upon Woo to produce evidence that:

- Racially, nationally or linguistically mixed marriages are less successful than marriages between partners of the same racial, national or linguistic group.
- The offspring of mixed marriages are less well adjusted and happy than the offspring of non-mixed marriages.

Amusingly, elsewhere in the same edition of the magazine, under the heading 'new snobberies', a cartoon showed two dark-skinned people watching two Europeans at some date in the future. One says to the other, 'Very sad my dear, not a drop of mixed blood in their veins!'

Larry Feign, an award-winning political cartoonist who is married to a Hong Kong Chinese woman, describes in his comic strip *The World of Lily Wong* what he considers to be an irreverent, affectionate look at life and love by the South China Sea. As Feign says, East meets West, rich meet poor, and woman meets man, often with disastrous or hilarious results. The cartoon ran in the *South China Morning Post,* Hong

Kong's leading English-language newspaper, in the late 1980s and the early 1990s.

The strip was also published in a book of the same name (Feign, 1993):

> *'Take a sweet, sassy, single young [Chinese] woman, her foreigner-hating father, a horse crazy brother, hawkers, politicians, elitist snobs, fortune tellers, department sales clerks, cadres from across the border ... and a bumbling foreign devil who just won't leave the girl alone ... put them together and what do you get ...?'*

In another Feign book, *Hong Kong Fairy Tales*, the American writes, 'Every great civilisation leaves behind a rich and varied repertoire of myths, legends, fables and fairy tales. Most of these end with a moral. Which explains why no such thing exists in Hong Kong' (Feign, 1994:1). One Hong Kong folk tale begins with a European male and a Chinese woman who lived sometime during the nineteenth century. They fell in love and wished to marry, but her parents refused him and would not give permission. The couple drank poison near a massive rock along Bowen Road on Hong Kong Island, and their love pact suicide has never been forgotten. Chinese people still visit what everyone now calls 'Lovers' Rock', especially on the 'Three Sixes' (三六): the 6th, the 16th and the 26th of the lunar month. *Yan Yuen Shek* (姻緣石) [The Rock of Predestined Marriage or Fate], shaped roughly like a phallus, ranks as one of the most important, archaic cult objects in the region. People looking for partners, others wishing to bear sons, and employees of the sex industry, all worship it.

Moving on to a rather different subject, novels have often portrayed Asian women as being sexually appealing and demure, and believers in simple and true love.

White Mughals recounts the early promiscuous mingling of the races in India, one of whom was James Kirkpatrick, the British representative to the court of the Nizam of Hyderabad, who in 1798 glimpsed a beautiful, young Mughal princess (Dalrymple, 2002). Falling in love meant facing opposition from all sides, and marriage meant converting to Islam. There are similar love stories from many parts of the world.

The British author Somerset Maugham (1874-1965) took a liking to travel. Graham Greene flippantly described Maugham's subjects as 'adultery in China, murder in Malaya, and suicide in the South Seas.' Wherever Maugham went, his writing was largely influenced by the times during which he wrote, and he often voiced the power dynamics between colonists and locals. His novel, '*The Painted Veil*' (1925), was set in Hong Kong and cholera-infested China and gives a good portrayal of the region at the time.

The American author Pearl Buck grew up in China, and her first language was Chinese, although she wrote her books in English. Her first book, *East Wind: West Wind* (1930), describes two marriages within one Mainland Chinese family: the sister is in an arranged and unhappy marriage, while, in contrast, her brother defiantly marries an American girl in spite of his parents' objections. *The Good Earth* (1931), is the Pulitzer Prize winning story of a humble Chinese farmer's rise to a wealthy landlord status. Professor Mimi Chan, author of *Through Chinese Eyes: Images of Chinese Women in Anglo-American Literature*, criticised the novel for its 'unbalanced account of life for women in China at the time' (Chan interviewed by Parry, 1989:5). She appreciates Buck's intentions were good, and that she wanted to let the world know more about Chinese women, but 'I cannot help feeling that she is somehow exploiting Chinese people.' Nevertheless, although perhaps exaggerated to a degree, *The Good Earth* does give a balanced account of China at the time.

Eurasian author, Timothy Mo, does not consider himself to be a Hong Kong writer, as he lived many of his formative years in England, and writes in English. With an English working class mother from Norwich, and a Chinese lawyer father from a fairly well-known, well-off Hong Kong family, Mo was born not only of a cross-cultural marriage, but also of two different socio-economic groups (Waters, 1995:12). His parents separated when he was two years old.

Interestingly, Mo's English mother had always thought her young son was too Chinese, and a primary school teacher in Hong Kong, according to Mo, used to say he was too English. On his way back to Britain at the age of ten, he says he had forgotten all his Cantonese by the time the ship had gone through the Suez Canal, or so he likes to recount. He led a British lifestyle, and became 'a true Brit' (his words). Although a champion boxer (not a Chinese martial arts practitioner it is noted), Mo is a small man who takes after his Cantonese father in appearance.

His first novel, *The Monkey King* (1978), won the Geoffrey Faber Memorial Prize at a time when there were few ethnic minority writers in the literati. Set in 1950s and 1960s Hong Kong, the debut novel chronicles a Cantonese family, particularly on the observations and experience of Wallace Nolasco, the Macau-born son-in-law.

Mo's second book *Sour Sweet* (1982) was short-listed for the Booker Prize and was adapted into a film. It also explores a Chinese family from the inside, this time also in London, through the eyes of a woman, Lily Chen, who prefers to live within the small Chinese-oriented realm of her family, than to have contact with the British society. Mo describes the Chinese society in London as:

> 'At the centre of 1960s London, the busy Chinese community lives by its precise and violent rules, flourishing like a spiky, brilliant crystal garden in the murky waters of Soho. Pitched into an alien city which is neither hostile nor friendly but very strange and very foreign, the Chen family prospers by deftly and sometimes incongruously blending tradition and opportunity, but no private family lives beyond the reach of the most powerful Chinese "family" – the triads' (Mo, 1982).

Richard Mason's *The World of Suzie Wong* (1957), with its western image of a Chinese bar girl in Hong Kong's Wan Chai district and its 'love conquers all' theme, not only became a bestseller, but it changed the international image of Hong Kong, and was said to have attracted a number of young

Western men into Chinese studies. A Broadway show and a film were made, both of which were banned in apartheid-era South Africa.

In a word, *The World of Suzie Wong* put Hong Kong on the map. Arthur Hacker, a retired civil servant, writes in *The Hong Kong Visitors' Book* (1997:204), 'what had been a delightful, sleepy, tropical, colonial backwater with a funny name nestling in the South China Sea, turned into a brash, harsh, garish cesspool of vice and depravity overburdened by appalling poverty.' An exaggeration, yes, but after *The World of Suzie Wong* was published, many more bars opened to cater to the increased number of American service men who came to the Colony on 'rest and recreation' from the war in Vietnam. Several bars had a girl who claimed to be the original 'Suzie' portrayed in Mason's story. In actuality, she was a composite.

Richard Mason, in 1955, deliberately visited Hong Kong for inspiration for a novel. Like his hero Robert, Richard mistakenly checked into a 'brothel,' as the tale goes (typical sensationalism!). He stayed there for four months. I remember the 'Luk Kwok' well, although the building Mason describes was demolished long ago, and a more modern one of the same name has seen built on the same site. Mason used to frequent the bar on the ground floor of the hotel which, in his book, he called the 'Nam Kok.' This is the description of the bar:

> In the Nam Kok are the providers of pleasure, the
> Chinese girls, outwardly indifferent to the men
> they entertain but each one a personality on her
> own. Amongst the girls is Suzie Wong, vivacious,

attractive, slowly showing more than professional
interest in the young Englishman who lives in a
cheap room in the hotel (Mason, 1957).

Around his paid work as a teacher at the British Council,
Mason conducted field work for his novel: talked with the girls
in the bar and with American sailors on shore leave. Mason
even once dined with the Governor, Sir Alexander Grantham.
According to Hacker, a considerable stir was caused when the
Governor's car pulled up outside the Luk Kwok Hotel to drive
Mason up to Government House for lunch.

The film part of Suzie Wong, the 'tart with the
heart', was played by the Eurasian Nancy Kwan. Her father,
architect H. K. Kwan, met her Scottish mother in the Astoria
Dance Hall in London's Charing Cross Road (Holdsworth,
2002:195). This did not go down well with the groom's family
in Hong Kong, and the couple were soon divorced.

Nancy Kwan brought the story to life, carrying herself
as a virgin while playing the part of a whore. In the end, true
love: Robert and Suzie marry. The heroine says:

'Go to bed with sailors – nothing happens inside.
Nothing happens to heart.' 'Go to bed with you
– everything happens. I love. I feel beautiful. I think
'my man'. You think 'my girl'. We belong.'

Chinese women are often stereotyped as oriental sirens
whose main aim is to please Western men, or to acquire rich
husbands. Professor Chan criticises James Clavell's well known
Taipan (1981), where 'May May is an outrageously compliant

sex-object who would offend the sensibilities of any self-respecting woman' (Chan, 1989:234).

Chinese women are also frequently seen as petite, soft, feminine, gentle, obedient and loving. Yet often sex and violence, coupled with the lure of the exotic, glamour and mystery, are added and woven into a work of fiction. In real life, some Chinese women are described as thermos flasks – cold on the outside and hot within, meaning assertive, strong-willed and hot-tempered. One middle-aged, Shanghainese who has lived in Hong Kong for most of her life, is fond of saying that in her natal family, the women always had the upper hand. 'My Shanghainese father was 'afraid' of my mother,' she told me.

It was often thought in the past that a Western man could not ever really get close to a Chinese woman. In the novel *The Sanctuary* by Anthony Cooper, a Western male character says, 'He knows no matter how much he loves his wife, he could never break through to her Chinese core. No non-Chinese ever can' (1984:223).

This view is linked to a stereotype of the Chinese woman as the witch, the killer, a woman with a cold, mean heart. The first Asian-American actress who became an international celebrity, Anna May Wong, who was born as Wong Liu Tsong in 1905, made over fifty films, spoke English, German and French, and was said to have the most beautiful hands in filmdom. Her peak was between the 1920s and 40s. Wong revealed that there were two extremes in the roles she played, the diabolical Dragon Lady, and the fragile Lotus

Blossom, from villain to victim.

After losing some critical roles to non-Chinese women actresses, Wong left the United States in the 1920s for Europe where, on the whole, they were far less inhibited about casting Asian actors (Mahoney, 2004):

> It's a pretty sad situation to be rejected by
> Chinese because I'm too American and by
> American producers because they prefer other
> races to act Chinese parts.

Yet in 1930, the British Board of Film Censors forbade English actor, John Longden, from kissing Wong on screen in *Road to Dishonour*. It was all right for him to sit at her feet, kiss her hand and hold her in his arms, but not to kiss her on the lips, however demurely (Gillingham, 1983:11). Love scenes between Americans and Chinese were also not permitted as a general rule.

There has been a recent surge of interest in Wong's career with the 1997 World Premiere of the play, *China Doll – The Imagined Life of an American Actress* which had its debut in New York at the Pan Asian Repertory Theatre. In 2004, the UCLA Film and Television Archive, and Hugh M. Hefner, founder of the Playboy Enterprises, presented a lecture and film series entitled *Rediscovering Anna May Wong*. In the same year, the Museum of Modern Art in New York City presented *A Retrospective of Chinese American Screen Actress Anna May Wong*, which screened six of her films and rare newsreel footage.

A Western stereotype of a sylph-like Chinese beauty,

may be a petite almond-eyed woman with long, smooth black hair hanging straight down her back, and wearing a tightly fitting cheung saam. If you ask a Chinese woman, she would probably say that the hallmarks of beauty include porcelain skin as clear as jade, a goose-egg shaped face, a small mouth, a high nose with a bridge, and double eyelids for a sense of increased size, high spirits, and more feeling and affection. She also traditionally values sleek, so called 'phoenix eyes', with over-arched, delicate, feathery eyebrows, as delicate as the moth's silken feelers, a wasp waist, a 'cockroach' (flat) tummy, with a body as slim as a willow tree. In old China, a woman over thirty was like 'used tea leaves' (爛茶渣) (*laan cha ja*).

Stereotypes are, after all, perfectly natural for all races. Many of us have met the philanthropic *tai tai* (太太) [wife], married to a well-off Chinese husband, who is possibly addicted to mahjong. Then, there is the *siu jer* (小姐) [common parlance meaning 'miss'], the ultra feminine, single woman looking for a rich husband, and, the Chinese *amah* speaking far too loudly. For one of his *South China Morning Post* columns in 2003, Tom Hilditch trawled the Lan Kwai Fong entertainment district in Hong Kong's Central District and asked Western men for their thoughts on the mystique of Chinese women. (Hilditch, 2003)

1   Chinese girls are conservative outside but in bed they're radical.

2   I just love their boutique size. My Chinese girlfriend makes me feel ten-feet tall.

3   Aging isn't a problem for Chinese women.
    They've got all those cosmetics and skin care
    products, and they know how to use them.

4   Chinese girls are so much more
    straightforward than Western women.

5   They are committed without being petty.
    My girlfriend doesn't mind if I watch
    football with the boys.

6   They are skinny and cute. They know
    the rules of love affairs, which is to follow
    wherever your man goes.

7   Maybe all Western men look the same to
    the Chinese, or maybe they just don't care.
    Otherwise, let's face it, how could an ugly
    guy like me ever hope to get such a beautiful
    girl back in the United States?

In *Through Chinese Eyes: Images of Chinese Women in Anglo-American Literature*, Professor Mimi Chan quotes from Harry Rickett's collection of stories and sketches of Hong Kong, *People Like Us* (Ricketts, 1977). This describes the break-up in the relationship of a 'shiftless' (as described by Chan, 1989:234) Western young man and a Chinese youth who comes from a rich, Chinese family. It typifies the 'love them, leave them' attitude that many Chinese perceive Westerners have towards Chinese. The following exchange is in a restaurant, at the time of their parting (Chan, 1989:234):

'Well, are you happy I'm going?' the girl says.

'What do you think?' the Western youth replies.

'I don't know. My friends told me Europeans have no feelings.'

'What else did they say?'

'That you get what you want, and then you don't want it any more.'

'Nice friends you have.'

'You don't know them.'

Whose fault is that?'

'I really loved you.'

'Would you like some more tea?'

He orders more tea and coffee.

'It's someone else, isn't it?'

'I don't want to talk about it.'

'Is it what I said about going out with other people?'

'You give me no freedom.'

Even today, when close friends of a Chinese woman hear that she is involved with a European, they frequently try to help her by attempting to specifically find out what sort of a person the man really is. Is he serious? Is he likely to leave you in the lurch? Can you trust him? How long is he staying in Hong Kong?

Other interesting viewpoints about Western-Chinese marriages are expressed in the books by the well-known, contemporary Chinese-American author, Amy Tan. Her first two novels, *Joy Luck Club* (1989) and *The Kitchen God's Wife*

(1991) are both stories revolving around the situation of the Chinese émigré mother and her more Americanised daughter.

> 'Sometimes I regret that I ever married into a
> Chinese family,' Phil said when he heard we had
> to go to San Francisco (Tan: 1991,15).

This highlights a concern that Europeans often warn friends about when they are contemplating marriage with a Chinese person, or any Asian. A typical expression used by Westerners is, 'You don't marry the girl, you marry the family.'

Which of these stories – fictional and from history – are echoed in the lives of the 81 couples in our survey? Are the stereotypes borne out?

voices of
eighty-one
east-
west
couples

my better half

No decent Chinese girl will marry you. All you can expect is a whore or a bar girl.

A clergyman in Hong Kong in the 1950s

How intentional was it for the 81 couples to marry someone from another culture, from another ethnicity? About half of the respondents of the survey said they had never made a plan to do so. The subject of marrying out never arose, they were totally open-minded, and ethnicity was not something they had ever considered while choosing their partner.

One European man did not want to marry someone who was not from a similar culture, but ethnicity was not an issue. In other words, to marry a 'westernised Chinese' was perfectly in order. A French woman had always felt it would be fine to marry a foreigner, but her Chinese husband had grown up with the view that he should marry his own kind. One woman wrote that even the marriage between her Swiss father and English mother in the late 1940s was at that time considered a mixed marriage. An Australian woman wrote:

Never thought of such an issue. Nor did we discuss

cultures. I just liked the Chinese man for what he
was unless looks can be considered part of culture?

And, a Chinese woman expressed herself this way:

I had no strong feelings about marrying either a
Chinese or a Westerner, although I had certainly
thought it might be quite exciting if I were to meet
and marry a foreigner. But I never really thought it
would actually happen.

In much the same way, an Englishman who married
shortly after World War Two in Hong Kong was not really too
concerned himself about marrying into another race, although
at that time, spouses of these marriages were frequently considered
as 'novelties' or 'curiosities', he said:

But I was aware in 1950 when we married, that
others [cross-cultural couples] *did have problems. I*
remember my [British] *father did until he met my*
wife for the first time.

This man did not have quite the same cause for concern
because, although he married at a time when feelings against
Western-Chinese marriages were still strong, he worked in the
Hong Kong Prisons Department where such marriages were
not so uncommon.

One English man insisted that meeting his wife was
purely a matter of chance, like many of life's key decisions, and
I am reminded of a visiting European lecturer at the Centre
of Asian Studies at the University of Hong Kong who said he
made all his important decisions with the aid of *shing booi* (聖

杯) [divining blocks]. **[1]**He seemed to be implying, with a smile on his face, that there was just as much chance of the decisions being successful that way. It is understood this lecturer was not in a cross-cultural marriage.

To many people in this survey, marriage was seen as a matter of individual compatibility. A British man said:

> *I come from a mixed Scottish-Polish family, which probably made it easier for me to accept different cultures. My Chinese wife was brought up and educated in the medium of English in a Western environment in Hong Kong, as well as in England to such an extent, that I doubt if she would have survived a relationship with a conservative Chinese man.*

Polish people certainly seem very adaptable and after World War Two, in which they fought valiantly with the Allies, many married European women. On the second point, if a European woman can marry a Chinese man and live happily ever after, why cannot a Chinese woman who has been brought up in a Western environment do the same?

The next two Chinese women present interesting views, or doubts, about marrying Chinese men. The first wrote:

> *I had a long-standing conviction I would not marry a Chinese.*

When queried, she said she did not know why, just that she felt that way, deeply, almost instinctively, and in fact, she has long been happily married to a Welshman.

[1] *These divining blocks are found in a temple altar. The blocks are tossed half a metre up into the air, and if both blocks land flat side down, the answer is 'no'. If both fall on the carved side, the gods are laughing at the question. When the blocks fall one carved side up and one flat side up, the answer is 'yes'.*

The second woman, married to a Canadian, told me:

My father and other Chinese men in the family used to fool around. One of my aunties used to say, 'If a husband is providing for his wife and otherwise behaving decently towards her, then she should not complain. I did not want that sort of marriage. I believe the behaviour of my own family members, when I was a girl, had some influence on me.'

The aunt's views were by no means uncommon years ago, when many Chinese men had concubines and 'underground girlfriends' (to use a Chinglish expression), and many women, not very well-educated on the whole, depended greatly on men for financial and other forms of support. Yet one may question whether this young woman is rather naive if she believes that few Western men womanise.

Some people 'marry out', consciously or unconsciously, as a form of protest, feeling that there is something wrong with their own culture and they do not want to be swallowed up by it. They may see themselves as a bit of a rebel. Some Chinese people, for instance, feel that their culture is too conservative, too patriarchal, too insensitive, and with an unsatisfactory marriage ideal (Fong, 1995:77). A Westerner, meanwhile, may want to escape certain aspects of the culture, such as over-materialism in the United States, and provincialism in the United Kingdom, perhaps.

To some respondents, a cross-cultural marriage is seen as romantic and adventurous, and spouses like to believe that true love can cross many boundaries, whether race, class, religion or age. Some may even believe that marrying one's own folk can bore, and that a foreigner can add spark to one's life, can make a person feel special, and can avoid tiresome routines.

One Cantonese woman, who is in the survey, confided in her friends long before she married her 'foreign devil' that she was more attracted to Westerners. Yet she firmly maintains that a Western-Chinese marriage is no different to any other kind of marriage. Like many Chinese women, she places great emphasis on romantic love grounded in mutual respect and equality.

Another Chinese woman in this survey said that, within her large circle of friends in the 1950s and 1960s, some had already wed Europeans or were hoping to. Nevertheless, not everyone within the circle felt this way. One woman was emphatic that she had not wanted to marry a Westerner because in the West, it would not be easy to engage *amahs* (媽姐) (domestic workers), and she herself would have to do the housework. This woman was tall and attractive, and her two aunts, acting as matchmakers, helped her to *dew kam kwai* (釣金龜) (fish for a golden turtle), that is, find a rich husband. She eventually married a man from a well-off *Chaozhou* Chinese family.

Much more recently, a young Chinese man said that he had always wanted to marry a European because he thought such a relationship would more likely be based on pure love. This impression probably came about due to the norms of old China, with arranged marriages and matchmakers.

An elderly European, long married to a Chinese woman said:

My late mother-in-law was a tiny woman for whom marriage was decided at the age of sixteen. After all, marriage was considered to be too important then for the decision to be left to youngsters. Choosing the right partner for one's offspring required a conscious, pragmatic choice. It was necessary to select a lucky day, and proper planning was needed.

Today, Chinese people in Hong Kong are much more likely to choose their own spouse. Parents or relatives may exert a certain amount of pressure if they feel the choice is not a good one, and may use the expression: 'Let wooden gates match wooden gates and bamboo doors match bamboo doors' (木門對木門，竹門對竹門).

George Wright-Nooth might have agreed. The late senior police officer wrote of being invited by some Chinese businessmen to an establishment in West Point, the old entertainment district on Hong Kong Island before World War Two (Wright-Nooth, 1994:16). There, he recalls how he met high-class call girls all wearing the *cheung saam* (長衫), a long, straight, clinging and elegant dress with a high collar and a slit along each leg up to the thigh, as previously described, a dress common in Hong Kong up until the 1950s and 60s. He wrote, 'I knew then that if this was all they could produce for the very wealthy Chinese, then Chinese women would never physically attract me.'

Meanwhile, an American man who completed a

questionnaire wrote, 'I "thought" I was not interested in Asian women!' He has now been happily married to a Hong Kong Chinese woman for some years. An Englishman, who previously served in the Royal Hong Kong Police Force, put the question of figure rather more forcibly, 'I like my women to have bums and breasts.' Another Western man disagreed, 'I go for Chinese girls. They have gorgeous, svelte bodies with soft, silky, unblemished, almost polished nether parts with little body hair.' (Chinese women with hairless mons veneris has been recorded.)

Some of the expatriates who 'fall' for a Chinese woman are the last ones you would expect to do so. A tall Shanghainese woman has always marvelled at the fact that the man, to whom she has now been married for many years, even 'chased after' her. 'He is so English! He is not a good mixer and does not get on well with Chinese. Can you ever imagine how he came to marry me, a Chinese?'

One 'true blue' Brit admitted that his attraction and marriage to a Chinese woman came as a surprise, and he remembers there were 'degrees of resistance':

> One Sunday afternoon in the mid-1950s, I recall
> clearly wandering around Repulse Bay quite perturbed.
> I realised I was becoming fond of my Chinese
> girlfriend. As a European who had fairly recently
> arrived in Hong Kong, I felt at the time that
> the habits and customs of the Chinese were so
> different to those of us Westerners that it would be
> inadvisable and difficult for me ever to marry a
> Chinese.

Here was a person who saw himself as 'pure' British (who are actually a mongrel breed of Romans, Saxons, Danes and Normans, not to mention Celts, Picts, Jutes and so on!). Four years later, after his mild culture shock led to a growing fascination with Chinese culture, the man married his beloved.

Over the past half century, with the effects of globalisation, the East and West have grown much, much closer. But in the 1950s, largely the first decade of marriages in this survey, Chinese families were large, divorce was a rarity, many Chinese men took concubines and even got a tax deduction for them, and couples generally did not hold hands, link arms or kiss in public. As for dress, upper and middle-class women wore the traditional *cheung saam* and many working class, middle and even upper-class men wore the *saam foo* (衫褲), a matching jacket and trousers. In a typical workplace, even Westerners and Chinese of more or less equivalent rank were rarely on first-name terms, and would rarely mix after office hours. It was therefore not easy for Chinese and Europeans to meet each other. A European police officer related to me that during a talk with a new intake of inspectors at a training camp in the 1950s, a clergyman said to the men, 'No decent Chinese girl will marry you. All you can expect is a whore or a bar girl!'

In the case of the 'true blue' Brit's marriage to a Chinese woman, her maternal grandfather's fifth wife warned her that Europeans tend to have a 'love them and leave them' attitude. Several other Chinese women had also been advised by friends not to marry Westerners. One Shanghainese woman, who is quite modern in outlook and had studied in England for many years, said to her daughter, 'All right, you can go overseas to study, but you must promise me you will never marry a foreigner.' Some Shanghainese, when they came to Hong Kong to escape the Communist Revolution of the late 1940s, also told their children that they must never marry Cantonese. In those days, when there were few divorces, the Chinese saying 'marry a dog, follow a dog' (嫁雞隨雞，嫁狗隨狗) very much applied.

Similarly, Westerners were warned by other Europeans that it was not advisable to marry Chinese, largely because the two cultures and lifestyles were so different. One Englishman who lived in Hong Kong in the 1970s said to me, 'I do not mix with Chinese outside work because they do not speak my language.' Another who was leaving Hong Kong when he retired said, 'I want to live among my own kind.' It is interesting to hear this Englishman's thoughts, followed by an American woman's:

> *I am a free thinker and am used to holding views different from the majority, therefore I am less influenced by others' stereotyped views of race or culture and more influenced by the character of a potential spouse. However, I would differentiate between marrying an Oriental, whose race is similar in status and appearance to Occidentals, and marrying a person of very dissimilar race, for example a Negro. My reason is that a white-black marriage would certainly result in some racial prejudice which would be an additional burden to the couple and their children. This doesn't mean I*

*would not marry a black person, but I would take
the likely social problems into account. My wife
grew up in Hong Kong, was attracted to Western
culture and was comfortable in the company of
Westerners in her professional roles. Therefore,
[her] marrying a Westerner was not a big surprise.
But it was not planned.*

*Before I met my Chinese husband, I held the
opinion that I might possibly marry into a
European family. However I never, ever, imagined
that I would marry into Chinese culture or any
other Asian culture. Before I met my husband, I
had never personally known anyone from an Asian
or African culture.*

Another British man and his Hong Kong Chinese wife
said that before they met in the 1980s, they did not hold any
views about whether they would or would not be prepared
to marry into another culture. They both also added, very
emphatically, 'The wife's mother did!' Nevertheless, when the
wife gave birth to what would be her mother's only grandson,
all was forgiven, and the strong views disappeared. Many old
fashioned Chinese still place great importance on having a son
to continue the family line, which seemed to be the case for
this couple.

Similarly, many young Chinese people living in Britain
take a very matter of fact view when looking at marriage. Some say,
'English girlfriends are fine, but not as wives' (Waters, 1995: 73).
Chinese men who are going steady with a Western woman are

frequently teased about losing control of their lives, turning their backs on their own culture, and becoming 'set in concrete'. Some genuinely fear that, with different priorities, the British wife will desire the kind of company and lifestyle that a Chinese husband is unable to provide. Likewise, one British husband said he sometimes felt that his Chinese wife of long-standing preferred the company of other Chinese people, even though he himself is quite 'sinicized' in many ways. He added that his wife has been reverting to many of her old Chinese ways as she has aged, that she seems to enjoy the company of Chinese more and Westerners less. Most of the couples interviewed in the survey seemed to have their own circle of friends of their own nationality to whom they could turn, if necessary.

The Chinese-American tennis player Michael Chang says in his book, *Holding Serve – Persevering On And Off The Court*, that his future wife must be of Chinese ancestry (Chang, 2002). 'Mom and Dad never said, "you must marry a Chinese".' As Chang was growing up in Southern California, a melting pot of race and nationality, he came to this realisation on his own. After several trips to Asia, Chang saw that Chinese culture is 'far bigger than little old me' and he became prouder than ever to be Chinese. He now has a deep yearning to learn more about his heritage and to pass it on to his children. Unless the 'Good Lord makes it otherwise clear,' Chang says he will marry someone of Chinese descent, probably a Chinese-American, like himself.

chapter two
chicken talking with a duck

I was told off by my husband for giving what he described as the British two-finger salute.

A Chinese woman in Hong Kong

The official language of the People's Republic of China is Mandarin. For 3,000 years, the language used a 'traditional' unabbreviated script – sometimes called 'complicated' – but after 1949, the written characters were abbreviated or 'simplified' in order to make the language easier to learn and use. Then, in stages and over several years, the People's Republic of China has spent a great deal of time and effort introducing the Pinyin system of romanising words and places, which is very commendable, instead of people having to rely entirely on Chinese characters. Traditional characters are still used in Taiwan, Hong Kong and among some overseas Chinese communities, and, although more difficult to master with a greater number of strokes, these characters are also more artistic with their greater connotative power. Simplified characters with their 'deleted parts' can appear 'skeleton-like' or even 'barbaric', according to one Chinese calligrapher.

Dialects and sub-dialects are still very much in use in China. It has been said that there are as many in the country as there are days in the year (Ball, 1903:180). Cantonese, which is spoken in southern China, is as unintelligible to the average northern Chinese as German is to the average English person, and should certainly be considered a 'language' in its own right, not a dialect, which is how it is frequently described. Some Chinese spouses in our survey speak Chaozhou, Fujianese, Hakka or Shanghainese, a few are native Mandarin speakers, while most of the Chinese spouses in this survey are native Cantonese speakers.

Generally speaking, the Chinese spouse in our study is far more proficient in English than the Western spouse is in Chinese. Of the surveyed Chinese men, almost all claim to be able to speak English in addition to Cantonese and Mandarin, but only two wrote they speak 'professional' English. Among the Chinese women, almost all claim to speak fluent English and Cantonese, and reasonable Mandarin. On the whole, a number of Cantonese people speak limited Mandarin, and then with a heavy accent, so that people in Mainland China have been known to say, 'I do not fear Heaven, I do not fear Earth, I'm only afraid when the Cantonese speak Mandarin!' To be fair, Mandarin standards have risen considerably in Hong Kong, with language learning on the rise since China's Open Door Policy of 1978, and since Hong Kong became a Special Administrative Region (SAR) of China, in 1997.

Some Chinese spouses speak very polished English and one Englishman wrote:

Some English wives may be disconcerted by the
fact that [my Chinese wife] *has a better English*
education and has a much better command of
English than they do. I believe in such cases they
appear less friendly because they actually feel insecure
and defensive.

Of the Western husbands and wives in the survey, only about 22 per cent, say, have a reasonable command of either Cantonese or Mandarin and, of these, only a handful report that they can speak with any degree of fluency. The remaining 78 per cent apparently have little more than a smattering. Only ten per cent can read Chinese, and only two per cent at a high level.

The fact that the Chinese spouse is more fluent in English is logical really, as people brought up in Hong Kong or in other cosmopolitan cities are invariably exposed to English, or can seek it out without too much effort. Most Hong Kong Chinese study English and other subjects in English at primary, secondary and tertiary levels of education. Conversely, many Westerners only study Chinese on a part-time basis, and most often only as an adult.

It can be said that if a person knows little of his or her partner's language, it limits cultural understanding and full knowledge of one' s spouse, and can signal a lack of respect. The Chinese have a saying that when two people speak different languages, it is 'like a chicken talking with a duck' (雞同鴨講). It is not just the language that is different, it is the habitat, too.

Even a basic level of skill in a language helps a person enter a society and broaden his or her reality. There is no doubt that Chinese, particularly Cantonese, is difficult to learn, and that a large percentage of the Westerners who do begin lessons end up abandoning them. I recall an Englishman who came to the University of Hong Kong to teach three European languages. His intention, he told me on the ship coming out in the mid-1950s, was to learn Cantonese in six months. He was, after all, used to learning languages. Some time later, when I met him again and asked how he was getting on, he sighed, 'I have given up trying to learn. It takes too much effort to get anywhere.'

Several Western husbands in the survey also gave up in frustration. One said he had tried to learn, but stopped, and survives on 'taxi Chinese'. Another just could not hear the differences in the tones. A third, another Westerner, admitted he would rather spend his limited spare time doing something else:

> *I know there is the argument that if you marry a Cantonese girl, you should learn the language. However, it is very difficult, and I don't believe most men think about the implications of marrying into a completely different culture and, added to that, Westerners expect the girl to move into their culture, which they often do before marriage. I myself have tried to learn Cantonese. However the methods of teaching were poor and, with limited time, I decided some years ago I'd rather play the piano.*

Not long after one respondent first came to Hong Kong, he

asked an office assistant in his best, newly learned Cantonese, to please go out and buy him a comb (梳). Instead the assistant came back with a padlock (鎖). To the untrained ear, both sound similar to *soh*, except that the sound for lock has an 'upper rising' tone and the sound for comb an 'upper level' tone. Another European Hong Kong Government civil servant arranged to meet some Chinese villagers for a business meeting on Monday, but the villagers turned up on Sunday. The high or low tone of '*yat*' in *sing kei yat* (星期日) determines whether it is Sunday (星期日) or Monday (星期一).

This man advised his fellow Westerners not to worry too much about mastering all nine Cantonese tones:

> *Even if every tone is not pronounced absolutely correctly, the other person can often still understand from the context what one means unless the person one is speaking to tries to be difficult. And, if you are understood, you are half way there. That is the main aim. After all, many Chinese with their 'Chinglish', do not pronounce English words clearly.*

Indeed, many expatriates who live in Hong Kong for any length of time have built in several Chinese words into their vocabulary, saying *choi sum* not 'Chinese broccoli', *char siu* not 'barbequed pork', and *long ngan* rather than 'dragon's eyes fruit'. Many Westerners may not even know the English translations!

Domestic helpers can have some influence on which language is spoken in the household. As one Englishman said, 'when we employed Cantonese *amahs*, my wife and I spoke a great deal of Cantonese at home. After the early 1980s, when we started to employ Filipina helpers, we spoke more English.'

I offer a personal anecdote. When I sat my second colloquial Cantonese examination in 1955, one of the interview panellists, Dr Irene Cheng, one of Sir Robert Ho Tung's daughters, said, 'You' re speaking "*amah* Cantonese".' There was something in what she said. I used to practise speaking in the evenings with my servant.

One's own line of work is another factor. A police officer on a beat in a mainly Chinese district learns Chinese much faster then someone in an office where most everyone speaks good English. One retired prison officer said:

> *I did four exams in colloquial Cantonese... and I have certificates to prove it. I also have a smattering of Chaozhou, Hakka and Hokklo, mostly swear words, mind you* (Maher, 2003).

Contact and involvement with the extended family also affects the language dynamic. One American woman wrote:

> *My Cantonese husband and I, and our children have always spoken English together. Our sons speak English to each other at home, but mostly speak Cantonese with my husband's parents. My husband always speaks Cantonese with his parents, while I speak a mixture of Cantonese and English with them.*

A European woman said that when her grown-up Eurasian children and other relatives settle down to a meal, the conversation usually switches back and forth between Cantonese and English, and then, a little later, the conversation generally stays in Cantonese:

> *I don't mind. Indeed I am often not even aware of the shift. But occasionally it annoys me, especially if I'm tired or the subject matter is one with which I'm not familiar, thus making it more difficult to follow.*

With English so prevalent in Hong Kong, the push for the Westerner to learn Chinese is often not great enough. And when a Westerner does try to speak in Chinese, many people answer in English, wanting to practice their own skills. Then there are some Cantonese who seem to resent being spoken to in Cantonese, feeling: 'Do you think I am so poorly educated that I cannot speak English?'

Obviously, handicaps exist with being mono-lingual, especially when trying to mix with one spouse' s family and friends. Someone can interpret, but there are limitations. Things may not come across in quite the same way, details go missing, and nuances are lost. The saying that 'translation is a thief' can all too often apply.

'I feel left out of some of the nuances of my husband's English, and frustrated when I cannot share with him things involving my Chinese language,' a Chinese woman said. Interestingly, her husband writes that his wife, who had lived in Canada for a number of years, used some North American English expressions and terms which he as a British person did not understand in their early days together.

One Australian woman, on arriving in Hong Kong in the 1960s with her Chinese husband who was born there, was thrown in at the deep end. During the day when he was at work, she was left with the in-laws and a house full of servants. The fact that she could not communicate properly with anybody in the household obviously caused misunderstandings and difficulties. It took time to learn Cantonese but, even today she admits she is not totally fluent. She always speaks English with her husband, and mixes Cantonese and English with the children.

Problems can also stem from cultural gaps and different ways of living and communicating. Early in the marriage of a British-Cantonese couple, the Cantonese wife was shocked at the explicit nature of her husband's views and his outspokenness during arguments. She opined that Chinese culture demanded concern for 'face' and that relationships were like 'crystal', easily shattered, and never able to be reassembled. The husband totally disagreed and argued that the rational, Western approach was that differences needed to be aired thoroughly, and reasoned out to identify behavioural adjustments, which both parties could accept as fair. Finally, the husband's views predominated, and his way of dealing with differences was used thereafter.

On another occasion, however, this same husband complained because his wife used Cantonese at the dining table with the children, thereby locking him out of the conversation. His wife responded that using Cantonese was spontaneous and came naturally, and that if he did not understand what was being said, then that was his problem! This time, her view was accepted.

A Chinese woman in Britain said she sometimes had difficulty with slang or colloquial expressions, such as 'Do you mind!' The multiple meanings can be difficult to distinguish. Cantonese can confuse, too, *keuk* (腳), for instance, is either 'feet' or 'legs'. Also, if someone says, 'There is no fog today,' the standard reply in English would be 'no' (no fog today). In Cantonese, the reply would be 'yes' (I agree with you that there isn't any fog today.).

A Chinese woman who was born and brought up in Hong Kong and later studied and now lives in the United States, said that when she first married her Caucasian husband, she tended to act in a Chinese way and criticise him and, to use her expression, 'put him down'. For example, if someone said, 'Your husband is very bright,' she, as a 'correct' Chinese wife, would say, 'No, he's not really.' While in old-fashioned Chinese etiquette this shows humility and modesty, in the West it is generally considered as demeaning and not providing encouragement. Similarly, if a person compliments a child and says, 'He's good looking,' the Chinese mother sometimes replies, 'He's very naughty.' In other words, the aim is to defuse the praise, which Cantonese often lavish excessively on each other, in a good-natured sense of play.

They may for example exclaim to a group of colleagues about a European: 'He speaks fluent Cantonese, you know.' In fact, both the speaker and the European know, and some members in the group may know too, that this is far from the case. The Europeans' knowledge of Cantonese is actually rather limited. Another example is when a Chinese couple invite people to a banquet, or at least quite a lavish meal. As the guests are leaving, the hosts might say what amounts to, 'We are sorry we have served you such poor food and have provided such poor service.' Everyone knows it is a bit of show, and a case of being over polite.

Several couples felt that, yes, they had language misunderstandings, but nothing really serious. One Western man felt relieved when he heard that a Shanghainese Chinese was also having difficulty in differentiating between 'buy' and 'sell' in Cantonese. Both are usually romanised as *maai*, but the tones differ. It remains that some Shanghainese who came to Hong Kong half a century or so ago have never really mastered Cantonese, while this Western man said he considered his Cantonese to be reasonably fluent:

> *I can generally get my message over. Nevertheless, I sometimes feel I am not really expressing myself well, and my personality is not coming across in the same way as when I express myself in my mother tongue. I cannot speak with the same authority and I feel certain restrictions. When I speak English, I know that my replies are more to the point. I am also more relaxed.*

He continued that when he was with a group of people speaking Cantonese, he is much more reticent.

An American man talking about his northern Chinese wife, said:

> *She gets upset when the children or I say, in*
> *Mandarin, 'yao bu yao' (要不要)* [do you or
> do you not want any?]. *It is rude when offered*
> *something to say, 'bu yao' (No, I don't want any.)*
> *One should never offer a guest or a friend the chance*
> *to say 'No'. One's tone of voice can also cause people*
> *to get upset sometimes. Since all Chinese dialects are*
> *tonal, the Western ear sometimes misinterprets the*
> *mood of the Chinese spouse.*

But similar situations can also occur in English, as a British man pointed out:

> *I may wish to make some constructive criticism*
> *about a dear friend. The words may sound harsh*
> *to my Chinese wife, but they are said with a*
> *note of concern in my voice to signify that we*
> *should perhaps provide support or help. I feel I*
> *am being considerate and compassionate, but my*
> *wife may simply hear the criticism and accuse*
> *me of heartlessness.*

> *There are other situations where difficulties*
> *may occur. My response to petty-officialdom, for*
> *example, or my willingness to complain, or my*
> *tendency to ask for explanation or justification*
> *of statements, which may seem innocuous*
> *to my wife, can lead to tension between us.*
> *Whether such examples are to do with culture or*
> *temperament, each of which is linked to a degree*

to the other, is debatable.

A Western man living in Australia contributed:

The Chinese often appear not to be paying full attention to what is being said; their thoughts seem elsewhere... I get told I don't understand from time to time but that might not be due to my not paying attention, but being slow in reaction compared with my 'lightning little Chinese wife'. I'm basically slower in everything I do. She is often too quick in response, in my book, with little thought and follow-up action.

A British man mentioned that English sarcasm and irony is generally not appreciated and is often taken at face value by the Chinese. Rifts can easily happen. Understatement, which contrasts markedly from the American tendency to exaggerate, is also difficult to follow. A Chinese woman wrote:

There have been misunderstandings between my husband and I due to differences between implied and literal meanings. For instance, 'Not too bad!' Typical English 'understatements' can cause frustration and irritation.

But then of course, Cantonese also abounds with expressions that are hard for outsiders – people from other areas of China, or Westerners. Someone may say, 'Melon fields, under the pear tree' (瓜田李下). Cantonese people know automatically that you should not arouse suspicion by bending down in a melon field or adjusting your hat under a pear tree: someone may think you are stealing.

Humour is one of the most difficult aspects of learning a language. British self-deprecating humour is often interpreted literally by Chinese, and this can cause misunderstanding. One Anglo-Chinese couple admitted they did not always laugh at the same things, for instance the Chinese wife said she did not always find comedies such as *Monty Python* particularly funny. 'On the other hand, there are things that we can laugh at together,' the Western husband assured.

Self-mockery also plays a part in English humour. British people in Hong Kong often call themselves *gwailo*, a colloquial expression for a Westerner which commonly translates as 'foreign devil'. [2]

Does difference in humour and in language - the alphabet versus pictograms and ideograms - shape the way Westerners and Chinese people think, talk, and laugh (Waters, 1998-99;2)? A bi-lingual person might well answer 'yes'. Psychologists, on the other hand, might find it hard to suppress a smile, and likely say 'no'. The character for 'family' (家) includes a 'roof' (茅) over the 'house' and 'pigs' (豬) on the ground floor (地), for a typical rural family in China highly values its livestock and shelters the animals within the home. That was – and remains – common practice in remote areas as many of us know. Chinese characters are frequently 'built up' in this way just as they are used together as compounds. [3] The Chinese have no single, simple ideogram for 'crisis' (危機). Their equivalent is to use the character for 'danger' (危) and the character for 'chance' (機), side by side, and this, in other words, means 'crisis'. These characters, incidentally, are said to

[2] To make the point again, when Chinese first saw the pale faces of Europeans in the Middle Ages they thought they looked like ghost (or devil) people.

[3] For an interesting discussion on this subject, refer to, *If Triangles were Circles: A Study of Counterfactuals in Chinese and English*, by Cynthia Hsin-feng Wu, published sometime during the 1990s, by Crane Publishing Co. Ltd, U.S.A.

have greatly intrigued President Nixon (Waters, 1991:3).

But talking of 'reasoning' and 'senses of humour', a middle-aged Shanghainese who has lived in Hong Kong almost all his life once said to me, 'I'll tell you a joke which tickles Westerners, but Chinese cannot really see the funny side of it' (Waters, 1998-99:24):

> *A barman and a customer were chatting in a bar*
> *when in came another man. He walked up the*
> *wall, upside down across the ceiling, and then down*
> *the wall the other side. He ordered a pint of beer*
> *which he promptly quaffed. He then walked up the*
> *wall, upside down across the ceiling, down the wall*
> *the other side and out of the bar door.*
>
> *'That was strange,' said the customer who was left*
> *standing at the bar.*

The Shanghainese man was right. I told this joke to many Chinese friends and acquaintances in English and in Cantonese, and none of them, even when it was painstakingly explained, laughed! Chinese humour can vary depending on wherever it is from, Guangdong, Hong Kong or whatever. But as a general statement, Chinese humour tends to be lowbrow and physical, not philosophical, and there is often a liberal inclusion of adult jokes. Mother-in-law jokes do not go down well though, as filial piety is important in Chinese society. One Cantonese wife said, 'The English like to "insult" their friends. They say such things as, Hello you cheeky devil!' Although she has a splendid command of English, she admitted she sometimes could not grasp the jokes her 'old' man told. Then again, Cantonese nicknames are often teasingly unflattering. To give just one example, of many, a well-known and well-respected late Hong Kong actress, who is overweight, is known almost exclusively as Fei Fei [Fat Fat].

One cannot really understand anyone who is more complicated than oneself. Certainly some people, and some nationalities, are more complex in their actions than others, and they may speak with varying levels of innuendo, subtlety and elaborate coded systems. Body language may also be a full language: posture, hand gestures (which are more common among southern than northern Europeans) and facial expressions (which are more pronounced for Europeans than for Chinese) such as frowns, smiles, grimaces, raised eyebrows, gazing upwards, and direct eye-contact, are three main areas. A gesture, a smile, a guffaw, or a touch, can each mean different things, including a 'yes' or 'no'. Unlike the written word, body language is not easy to look up in a dictionary.

The most frequent emotions in facial expressions, as a general statement of cultures as a whole, are anger, disgust, fear, happiness, sadness, and surprise (Nicol, 2004). A smile is effective body language with just about any nationality, and laughter also need not be learned. But when the Bahinemo people of New Guinea first saw American people, they viewed all their faces as angry. In Chinese culture, too much eye contact can be construed as bordering on the confrontational, while in the West, not looking a person in the eyes can often be interpreted as dishonesty. If Chinese people wish to signify themselves 'count me in', for example they may point directly to their nose, while pointing to the chest is the Western way. Sportsmen in the West, such as boxers or football players, often fold their arms when they are having their photographs taken for the masculine look, but to the Chinese, this pose ordinarily communicates resistance and non-cooperation. Americans are fond of putting their arms around people when, in so many cases, this is not an accepted Asian practice; it is often seen as being too intimate. Muhammad Ali even went so far as to kiss a fifteen-year old girl on his visit to Afghanistan in 2002. Interestingly, however, same sex friends walking arm in arm is far more commonplace, and accepted in Asia, than it is in the West.

It is sometimes said that the Chinese are inscrutable, but actually they use many expressions. A Chinese girl, or woman, putting her tongue out is usually considered cute, whereas in the West it is seen as rude. When she laughs, she covers her open mouth (seen as unsightly) with her hand. This reminds me of the saying for laughter, 'See teeth, do not see eyes' (見牙唔見眼), and 'Eyebrows come, eyes go' (眉來眼去) to signify that a boy and a girl are 'making eyes' at each other.

While dealers in the Jade Market of Hong Kong signal prices to one other in a secret sign language, all Cantonese people in fact use hand signs to indicate numbers. Numbers up to ten can be signalled on one hand, for instance, 'six' is communicated by clenching one's fist and extending the thumb and little finger. One Chinese woman who took part in the survey wrote:

I was told off by my husband for giving what he described as the British, two finger salute when all I intended to signify was the number two!

This 'salute', with index and middle fingers forming a 'V', in British 'body language' means more or less, with a slight movement of the hand up and down, 'Get lost!' or much worse! It is, in fact, very similar to the 'V for Victory' sign introduced by Sir Winston Churchill during World War Two. The palm of the hand is made to face the viewer in the 'V for Victory' sign, while the back of the hand is made to face the viewer in the rude gesture.

Another Chinese woman, long married and very westernised, wrote:

My husband's more flamboyant (and probably Celtic-influenced) body language and tone of voice is occasionally misinterpreted by me, especially his gestures and comments about other drivers! In turn, my unwillingness to be embarrassed or to lose face is sometimes misinterpreted by my husband as an obsession with formalities and appearances.

An American husband wrote about his northern Chinese spouse:

My wife is a teacher and expects a much higher level of respect than a teacher in the United States. This frequently is a cause of misunderstanding. Lord help any student who takes off his or her shoes in class. The Western custom of students assessing and marking their teachers performance drives her nuts.

Meanwhile, she finds it rude when her husband or their children point with their fingers while speaking, and I too remember that during my childhood in England, I was also corrected and on occasions was told forcibly, 'It's not polite to point!'

How one raises one's children is a real test of any marriage, and particularly a 'mixed marriage.' There is a natural desire for parents and grandparents to want their children to share their language, and many Eurasian children in the survey can indeed speak both English and Chinese in spite of the fact that the majority of the children's parents do not speak both languages fluently. In a large number of the cases, English is the main and the only language spoken by the father. This bilingualism was achieved because, at the same time, a great deal of everyday conversation happened between the mother and children in Chinese. Written Chinese, however, remains weak for many of the children.

One British-Cantonese couple gave this estimate of the scenario, which is not atypical:

- Chinese wife switches from English to talking in Cantonese to children about 40 per cent of the time.
- Children speak to each other in Cantonese about 40 per cent of the time.
- English father speaks to wife and children in English one 100 per cent of the time.

Other couples brought up their children to speak English almost entirely. Indeed, in one or two cases, Western fathers seemed to discourage the learning of Cantonese. In other cases, parents seemed to take the view that it was difficult enough to master one language, let alone two. I recall one English father, talking about his Eurasian daughters, 'They are English!' He wanted them to be brought up accordingly.

Some research, especially in the first half of the twentieth century, claims that bilingual children have a more limited vocabulary and that certain aspects of 'intelligence', creativity for example, is affected (Romano; 1988:128,129). Yet, others argue that bilingualism in 'pillow talk', when a Western spouse is half awake in bed and utters something in Cantonese in the middle of the night, opens up new pathways of connections to the brain. This was the old argument with learning Latin and Greek. It sharpened one's grey matter.

A Western man, a fluent Mandarin speaker, recalled how for the first six years of marriage, he and his northern Chinese wife raised their children entirely in Mandarin. Consequently, it was necessary to 'pull a number of strings' to enter his eldest son into an international school in Hong Kong. When the boy grew a bit older and 'learned' his father was 'not really Chinese', he never spoke to his father in Mandarin again! The father has since spoken to the children in English, while the mother generally still speaks to them in Chinese, and this is 'accepted'.

Sometimes children complain about having to learn a second language. They may feign embarrassment among their peers and refuse to answer their parents in Cantonese as an act of defiance. Children do not like to be different: if Cantonese or English is not spoken among their peers, they do not like to speak then. In a British school, even an American or Australian child might try and adopt a British accent. In our survey, most of the Eurasian offspring had apparently picked up colloquial Cantonese rather naturally, and had no real difficulty adjusting at school because of language skills.

A Danish girl, Hannah Kvan, who lived for a time on Cheung Chau Island in Hong Kong spent most of her time with Chinese playmates. She easily picked up Cantonese with perfect tones and won a competition in the 1970s organised by 'Radio Television Hong Kong' for the best Cantonese-speaking foreigner. Her clergyman father told the author that Cantonese was really her first language. As for many of the Eurasian children whose British fathers were wardens at Stanley Prison and elsewhere, the same applied to them.

A few Western-Chinese couples in Hong Kong sent their children to schools where the lessons were conducted in Chinese. As a general statement, it seems that, when the mother is Chinese and when some Cantonese is spoken at home, Eurasian children have little difficulty at school, and grow up entirely bilingual. However, one American mother felt that:

> *Many of the teachers looked down upon our sons because they were not one hundred per cent Chinese. Teachers' attitudes collectively seemed to be, 'Who do you think you are that you can come and succeed in our school?'*

Similar problems can apply to children overseas. In the early 1960s, a seven-month old Chinese girl was abandoned in a squalid doorway in Kowloon, Hong Kong. She was taken in by an orphanage, adopted, and then lived in England from age three onwards, first in the South and then in the Midlands, in two districts with small Chinese populations. Nicole grew up as a 'banana': a person with Chinese features but with a Western lifestyle, in this case, with the typical English frowns and grins. Because she was 'different', Nicole was sometimes bullied and ostracized at school, and this made her ashamed of her ancestry. She made a conscious decision to act as English as possible and to emulate her peers. When she was a teenager, she went to Hong Kong for a holiday with her English mother. Some taxi drivers and waiters snubbed her and grew hostile: 'Why you no speak Cantonese?' Eventually Nicole said, 'Let's go home to England, Mummy!' Only as an adult did she become inquisitive about, and comfortable with, her roots.

Like Nicole, a Chinese woman named Lucy was raised in England. And, like Nicole, she encountered prejudice. She recounts when she got the role of Portia in *Julius Caesar* at Bristol Old Vic. 'A critic said, "It doesn't matter about the language. If one is not white, forget it!"' And when her Chinese boyfriend took her home to meet his parents, they were really chuffed that at last their son had met a nice, real Chinese girl. All went well until she opened her mouth! She had a broad, west-country accent!

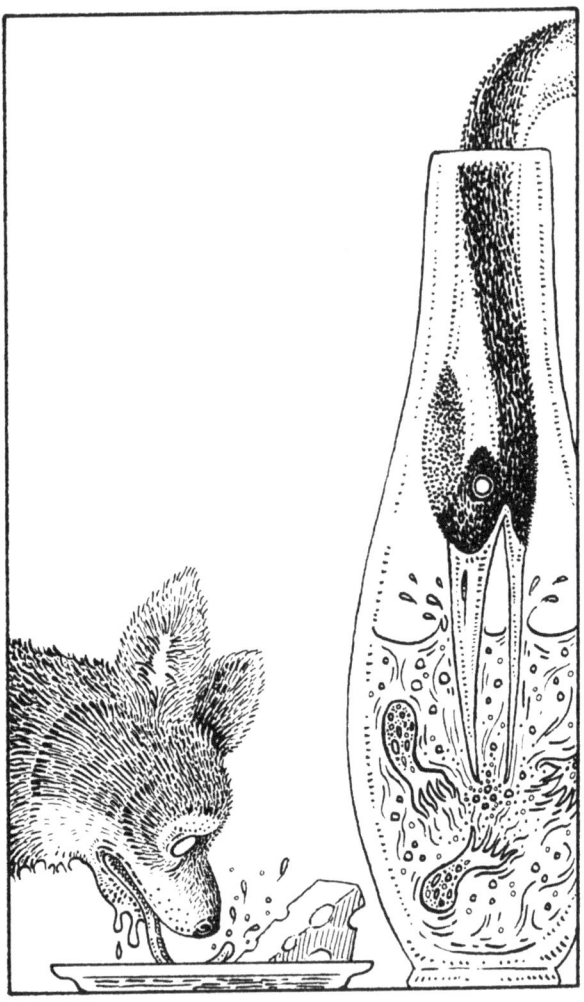

one family
two kitchens

The only thing I draw the line at is exotic seafood, like
sea slugs and octopus. Ugh! All those legs.

A Scottish man

Smells, tastes and the appearance of food are all
important in Chinese culture, as the well-known scholar, Lin
Yutang, (林語堂) once wrote in the 1930s: 'What is patriotism
but the love of food we ate as a child?' This could, of course,
be chicken feet, hamburgers, pig's blood,[4] black pudding,
or fish and chips.

Like the French who speak of *l'odeur de male* or *parfum
de femme*, Chinese people speak of old men's smell (男人味) and
women's fragrance (女人香): what we eat affects body odour.
People from India and the Middle East tend to consume a lot
of the pungent cumin seed that passes into perspiration giving
a certain smell. Some Americans and Europeans eat a good deal
of meat and dairy produce which can result in a considerable
amount of sweat with high levels of butyric acid. Some Chinese
find these smells distasteful, even 'repulsive'. The Cantonese
saying, *chow kwai* (湊鬼), refers to a woman who is dating a

[4] In Cantonese, 'pig's blood' is normally called 'pig's red' which sounds more acceptable. It is not unlike the minced pork fat and pig's blood 'black pudding' of northern England.

Westerner, with the connotation that she is nestling with a foul smelling foreign devil. This derogatory remark was more common when I was courting fifty years ago than it is today.

The high life expectancy in a frenetic city like Hong Kong says a great deal, many believe, for the health giving properties of Chinese cuisine where food ends and 'medicine' begins is unclear. Chinese classify food into groups such as 'heating' and 'cooling', with some groups fortifying the system, others acting as aphrodisiacs, and so on. One European man in the survey said he does not believe, as his wife does, that soup and ginseng are 'cure alls', nor that eating 'hot' (燥熱) or 'cold' (寒涼) foods necessarily makes one unwell. (Lai, 1978:11).

Food preparation and table manners also vary considerably from country to country, as well as within large countries like China, too. English and American children are frequently told, 'Keep your elbows off the table' while French people consider it correct to keep one's hands in full view, to avoid any monkey business under the table, so they say! Traditionally, Koreans never lift the rice bowl off the table, and Filipinos eat with their hands. Wheat is a staple in northern China, and rice in the south.

The language of Chinese food takes time to learn. Symbolism abounds (Watson, 1987:38). At the Lunar New Year, for example, it is important to eat *faat choi* [hair vegetable] (髮菜), if one wishes to make money in the coming year, and to serve a chicken complete. 'Have head, have tail' (有頭有尾) means that everything has to have a beginning and end, and in this case, a successful result. At the Mid-Autumn Festival, when the moon is full, round food is eaten, from mooncakes to pomelo. The longevity noodle speaks for itself.

For Chinese, a pair of chopsticks suffices for just about any dish. A German woman in our survey said that her Chinese husband preferred to eat any cuisine with chopsticks and that, she was annoyed when he used them even at Western restaurants. Perhaps he was following the advice of the scholar Lin Yutang, who once wrote that food tastes better with ivory chopsticks and porcelain bowls than with metal tableware.

One couple mentioned that when they were married in 1960, they were each given a pair of ivory chopsticks. 'Chopsticks' in Cantonese is *fai tze* (筷子) which sounds similar to 'quickly [bear] sons'. A *chi kwo* (慈菇) was another gift, a vegetable which looks uncannily like a penis and a scrotum which symbolised a wish for fertility.[5] Two bowls were also presented, one with a [male] dragon on it for the husband, and one with a [female] phoenix for the wife. The bowls signify 'may you never go hungry', for China has been racked by famine at many intervals over the centuries. Another wedding present might be two lotus roots placed side by side, decorated with a red, lucky, paper charm. When the roots are cut open, thin and long strands join the two separated pieces, signifying the ties to bind the bride and groom for a long, long time.

Incidentally, how a person holds their chopsticks is supposed to be a guide to where their future spouse will come from. If they hold their chopsticks right at the end, it

[5] *Some Chinese people I have interviewed have never heard of this custom. Among other things, the chi kwo was a wedding gift from our Cantonese amah, who came from a rural county in Guangdong Province.*

143

signifies that their partner will come from a long way away. Conversely, if they hold their chopsticks more towards the middle, that means their future spouse will live not far away.

One woman respondent said that compatibility in intercultural marriage depends as much on smelly, Shanghainese, fermented bean curd as anything else! Another joked, 'How can you expect Chinese to be able to appreciate Western culture when they do not like cheese!' And, what about Westerners not appreciating a nice, juicy chicken foot! A European husband remarked that his Chinese wife had not embraced the English custom of partaking of steak and kidney pie nor had he [the husband] managed to face up to chicken's feet. **6**

This British man told us this:

I find my family's love of chicken feet amusing and pretend to be horrified even though my mother was a British farmer's daughter and also ate chicken feet.

If fact, chicken feet appeared several times in the survey. An overseas Chinese who was not brought up on such delicacies in England, said that to her surprise she quite enjoyed them when she finally tried them. Many Chinese people believe in the saying, 'Eat the part to nourish the part' (以形補形) even if they do say it with smiles on their faces. Will eating chicken feet 'nourish' one's feet and create a better hiker?

Most couples said that they ate both Chinese and Western

6 *Many Chinese dislike the 'high' smell of steak and kidney pie. Similarly, they object to the 'gamey' taste of pheasant after it has been 'hung', as is common in England. All food, they strongly believe, should be eaten fresh.*

food, with proportions varying from half and half, to 65 per cent and up to 80 per cent Chinese. 'Chinese' food seemed to imply mainly, but by no means entirely, Cantonese food. In fact, seven couples said they ate almost entirely Cantonese food, with an occasional Western meal. A few couples disputed over proportions, with the wife saying they ate 'half and half' and the husband claiming they ate more Chinese food.

'Fusion cooking', with say Chinese food cooked to suit Western tastes, has become popular, although purists frequently object to it. In fact, some even object when for instance Cantonese and Shanghainese dishes are served at the same meal. Many couples said they occasionally eat Indian, Japanese, Thai, Indonesian, and other ethnic food. Location, also comes into the equation. One American-Chinese family writes:

> In our Hong Kong home, we almost always eat
> Cantonese food for lunch and dinner. In our home
> in the United States, we usually eat American food
> for the same meals. In both places, for half of the
> time we eat Chinese breakfasts (noodles and congee)
> and for the remainder we eat American breakfasts
> (eggs, pancakes and so on).

Purchasing necessary ingredients for cooking Chinese food is not always possible in the West. One Caucasian husband and his Hong Kong Chinese wife, who have lived in America for many years, said they occasionally have a Cantonese meal but eat 'mostly hybrids', pasta with Chinese sauce or rice with American toppings. This came over very much as American style living, with an emphasis on speed in preparation. Likewise, one European-Chinese couple living in fast-paced Hong Kong said they ate two-thirds Western and one-third Chinese, although most meals were not really representative of a particular cuisine and were 'hastily assembled'. 'We love microwave!' Another couple who 'ate mainly Western' but also Japanese, Thai and Indian, added 'Chinese food, which we both like, is more of a hassle to cook.'

An American man says that habits have changed gradually as he and his wife have aged:

> We almost always eat northern Chinese food. As
> we have gotten older, the occasional Western meal
> becomes rarer and rarer.

There are a small number of Westerners who do not like Chinese food, and there were three couples in the survey who eat mainly Western food. Some Westerners are allergic to monosodium glutamate (MSG), while Shanghainese tend particularly to like the flavouring. Some Chinese restaurants advertise 'no MSG', including the best restaurants in Sydney.

One Englishman dislikes the way a cooked chicken is served chopped up: he doesn't like to 'negotiate' the sharp bones. Meanwhile, a Chinese man and his European wife created a blend:

> I would say [we eat] mainly Western style but often
> with Chinese ingredients. For example, most of the
> time my wife and I each have our own separate
> plate of food, for example a piece of fish with a heap

of vegetables. We do not use chopsticks and eat from the common pot.

Meanwhile, these two couples cannot always find a compromise and often eat different meals:

We have a 'mixed kitchen'. My wife does not like Western food, so she always eats Chinese. I almost always eat Western. It is a bit troublesome, but there it is.

We often eat Western dishes but with rice rather than potatoes. My [Chinese] *wife frequently cooks something Western for me and Chinese for herself. Most considerate, but that is her. In family gatherings, we prefer Chinese dishes partly because they are less expensive and more predictable.*

Many Westerners living in Asia do become very partial to rice. When 'Old China Hands' go on holiday to the West, some of them miss it quite a lot. Yet, according to accounts of Westerners who were in Japanese prison camps, many never really got used to a rice based diet (Roland, 2001:128).

Most respondents appear to eat both meat and vegetarian dishes. One father says:

Our family is equally happy with Chinese or Western food and my wife is expert at cooking both. I evangelise about vegetable intake, and minimizing white bread and junk food. The kids experiment with cooking but always with health in mind. The main emphasis is on a healthy diet that

*is cost effective. Chinese? Western? Who cares? We
are liberated from cultural conformity.*

One Scottish husband eats many Chinese foods, but avoids
others:

*We run a predominantly Chinese kitchen with only
a few Western meals. This includes snake in winter
and all the rest of the goodies that seem strange to
most gwailos. The only thing I draw the line at is
exotic seafood, like sea slugs (海參) and octopus (八
爪魚) … Ugh! All those legs* (King, c. 1996:8).

Another Western man eats Chinese, all-inclusive:

*I enjoy sea slugs, octopus, de-boned duck's tongues,
congealed pig's blood and rice worms. They're
something different. Rice worms are caught in the
paddy fields. They have to be cleaned thoroughly
and salt is used and other ingredients added.
When a small group of us go over the border into
China from Hong Kong, when a Chinese friend
orders dog meat, it's interesting to see the reaction
among the Europeans. Personally, I eat and enjoy
it. After all, they are bred for the table. Many of
my Western friends cannot bring themselves to
touch Western culturally forbidden foods.*

A Chinese woman touches on this:

*My English hubby disapproves if I eat endangered
species, such as bird's nest or shark's fin soup.*

A famous Hong Kong Eurasian who was ill just after

World War Two was said to have been nursed back to health on breast milk, which might be seen as an ethical violation, and in 2003, a restaurant in Hunan Province in China was fined for serving mother's milk products (*South China Morning Post*, 2003).

The Chinese, in particular the Cantonese, are often criticised for their all-inclusive eating habits, as this poem illustrates (Parker, 1995:67):

> With their little pig eyes and their large pig tails
> And their diet of rats, slugs and snails,
> All seems to be game in the frying pan
> Of that nasty feeder John Chinaman.

But then I have dined with Chinese who refuse to eat beef. 'The water buffalo is man's best friend. He helps us plough the fields.' Yet they readily eat dog meat. Who is to say what is permissible?

in-laws, family and friends

Every man lives within ten miles of his mother-in-law.

A Western saying

Among the couples in the survey, there were some very firm, amicable relationships with the in-laws, and with spouse's friends; in other instances, not so friendly. Respondents admitted they were not always comfortable in the company of their spouse's relatives and friends due to language difficulties and customs, and some people dreaded having to mix with people 'on a different wavelength'. Yet, a large number of couples in the survey said they had both Western and Chinese friends, and that they had surmounted any problems with in-laws and other family members.

A number of respondents said that, if any dissension existed, much of it was normal 'wife to mother-in-law stuff'. The Chinese believe that 'two tigers cannot live on one mountain', although one Anglo-Chinese couple in England maintain that the wife's mother still tries to control the family from 8,000 miles away! The wife in turn, is surprised at the few family ties her English husband keeps.

Certainly family dynamics and the code of conduct for Chinese extended families often bring surprises. A parent not attending the funeral service of his own child left one English husband shaking his head in disbelief, yet many Chinese believe it is not advisable for 'whiteheads to go to the blackhead's funeral' (白頭人送黑頭人) *(baak tau yan sung haak tau yan)*. The fear is that an elderly, white-haired parent may be so distraught that they may be unable to bear the pain; 'ill may befall them', such as a heart attack. Similarly, a British husband is sometimes advised by his Chinese wife against attending a funeral during, for example, the month of his birthday. Happy events should not clash with the sad, or adverse effects can happen.

The survey indicates that Chinese tend to involve members of their family in their own personal affairs more than Europeans do. A Caucasian wife wrote that when she came to Hong Kong in her mid-twenties, she felt her in-laws' actions were 'controlling and interfering', but now that she understands Chinese culture better, she knows they were just 'interested and caring'. In fact, she now adopts a similar approach towards them and her own elderly parents, too. She continued that she felt Chinese siblings can be very competitive, not only concerning work and financial status, but also concerning the achievements of their children. She has kept a distance from her husband's siblings:

I have noticed resentment over the years, by relatives,

*regarding my children and their bi-lingual skills
and the good schools they have attended. Also there
was resentment when I didn't work and stayed at
home to look after the children myself. There were
times when I was treated as if I didn't work because
I wasn't well educated or capable of doing so. This
wasn't my imagination. They were not at all subtle
about it. I realise some of this comes from cultural
background but it hurts just the same. I would say I
am not close to my Chinese husband's siblings, and I
would not like to rely on them for anything.*

In the traditional Chinese family, members have clearly
defined roles, whether it be the grandmother or the eldest son,
and to a large extent all are judged, and judge themselves, by
how everyone fulfils their own responsibilities (Nicol, 2003).
The traditional role of the oldest son is to provide for his
family in the future, and after getting a good job, he is to help
the family, such as financing younger brothers' education.
Doing well by one's family is as important to the Massachusetts
Institute of Technology trained engineer as to the aged hawker
selling chestnuts on a Hong Kong pavement on a winter's
evening. 'Do your best to conquer selfishness.' 'Do not rock
the sampan.' 'Always respect tradition which morally begins
at home.' It almost boils down to every family for itself, and
almost every family believes that a high rank is desirable,
coupled with the prestige it carries.

Perhaps the main problem facing many Westerners,
when they become members of a Chinese family through

marriage, is communicating with Chinese in-laws, as many of the older generation do not speak much, if any, English. There were other Western respondents who could speak some Cantonese, but complained of problems communicating with in-laws when they spoke Cantonese too fast, not clearly, or when they discussed complicated subjects.

Of course, a similar situation exists for a Chinese spouse when parents of, say, their German or French partner, speak neither English nor Chinese. One Chinese man regrets he cannot communicate with his German in-laws. 'Learning German is too difficult.' In spite of such problems, a number of Westerners said they generally get on well with their in-laws. Those Westerners who spoke 'some' Cantonese said they were not fluent enough, which meant that the wife or someone else had to act as an interpreter in order to 'work around problems'. This self-inadequacy 'bothered' some Westerners. But another said, 'I have no problems with my in-laws. We cannot converse!' Another husband said, 'My wife's mother does not speak English, but we smile a lot!' 'Marital relationships are founded on love and trust,' said one Englishman, 'and, in spite of lack of communication with my in-laws, there is no lack of understanding between my wife and I.'

One Australian wife who in the traditional way lived with her Chinese husband's family, most of whom did not speak English, agreed that difficulties arose in her first transitional years of living in Hong Kong:

There were many adjustments and hurdles to

overcome, especially when my husband was at work. Inability to speak the language was (looking back) the major problem for me as that made everything escalate into having problems in following instructions and traditions. A basic conversation had to be guessed or ignored, or it meant just going along with whatever one imagined one should do and not knowing what was going to happen next. My Chinese husband always said, 'Why need there be any problem?' He has always been kind, generous and nice to my family

This European woman left a very Western lifestyle to move to Hong Kong, and live with her husband's family in 1970 for a total immersion into Chinese language and culture. To put it mildly, 'It was not easy.' The mother-in-law considered it 'her house' and that she had the right to interfere in any family member's business and to go anywhere, into any room, if need be, without knocking. Living the Chinese way also meant other frustrating things, like different table manners, the television being switched on all day and to a Chinese channel, and getting used to such cumbersome terms as 'number six uncle' (六叔) [*Luk Suk*, father's younger brother]. It was so hard going that the wife left and went back to Europe. Her husband went to bring her back, in spite of his mother telling him not to. Finally, the wife agreed to return, providing the couple could live on their own. The arrangement has worked amiably, and over the years, she and the children have learned to speak Cantonese, although she is the first to admit she is not fluent.

This is certainly not the first time a mother-in-law has wrecked, or nearly wrecked a marriage. It happens everywhere. In another case, a Japanese husband would tell his English wife, 'My mother says so and so …' and he would want his mother's instructions followed. Everything revolved around his family, particularly his mother. The wife realised the relationship must change or come to an end. They ended up divorcing.

However, another Western wife with a Chinese husband wrote:

> We were lucky to be financially independent and not to have to live with in-laws, as many newly married mixed couples do. We have also always benefited from having enlightened, accepting parents and relatives who welcomed our children without prejudice once they had got over the initial surprise and shock of our cross-cultural marriage.

In another case, an Anglo-Scots husband partly blames any rifts with his wife's family on his own inability to learn Cantonese, in spite of having attended eleven courses. Differences in culture were frequently blamed when in-laws and relatives criticised their marriage:

> My family clearly gave preference to boys over girls. This was unacceptable to us. My husband believes that if he had been fluent enough in Cantonese, he would have won over my relatives to his rational and moral way of thinking, and so he partly

blames himself for the rift.

One reason sons and grandsons have been considered important in Chinese culture is because only they can 'buy water' at the funeral of the father, a very symbolic ceremony and an act of great filial piety during which the father's corpse is 'washed'. In a traditional Chinese village, the eldest son would go to the nearest stream, drop in three small copper coins, and bring back this water for the ritual. For the urban Chinese, it may be little more than a symbolic dab of water on the father's forehead. In the old days, some Chinese fathers who only had daughters might take a concubine for a better chance of a son being born (Waters, 1991:116).

A European wife valued being briefed by her husband, the oldest son in his family:

> *The wisest thing my Chinese husband ever did*
> *was to explain to me clearly from the beginning*
> *the family system and his position as the eldest son.*
> *It became apparent very early on that father took*
> *priority over everyone else, including me. I lived*
> *in Hong Kong for six months before we married,*
> *and I spent a lot of time with my Chinese mother-*
> *in-law who was a dear lady. She and I became*
> *close friends.*

One interesting point that clearly emerged from our survey was that some Chinese grown-ups and children alike, and even some very westernised Chinese, still *kow tow* (叩頭) **7** to their parents at Chinese New Year, birthdays and so on. Even some Western women *kow tow* to their in-laws, as did the

7 *A ceremonial gesture in which a person kneels before senior family members and touches his or her head to the floor.*

Austrian Traute Shaw at the time of her marriage into the Sir Run Run Shaw family, a wealthy and influential Shanghainese family living in Hong Kong (Shaw, 2004:127). As Traute said, she accepted she had married into a totally different culture:

> It was an experience I find difficult to describe, moving for me and fun for everyone else. Mother and father immediately helped me back on my feet. Then again on my knees, as is the custom, I served them and all the other in-laws a cup of tea. I was told I was now accepted into the family by this ritual and could only pray I had made a good impression.

Meanwhile, one middle-aged, more modern Chinese man told me with great emphasis, 'I would never expect my sons to *kow tow* to me.'

Sometimes problems arise when a European and a Chinese meet, marry and live in the West, and then resettle in Asia. 'My husband is completely different to how I remember him [in the West],' is a typical remark. Maybe Chinese, men in particular, want to demonstrate to their relatives and friends that they are still Chinese at heart, and that living in the West cannot change their self-identity. Sometimes they become 'born again Chinese' and if the wife finds the going tough, he might say, 'Sorry about that, I'm Chinese. Take it or leave it.'

One Westerner, like a number of others in the survey, said his in-laws had lived in the West for many years and were very 'Canadianised', so cultural problems did not really exist.

Nor did they for many other spouses, whose in-laws lived several thousand miles away. Yet for some, this western saying applied: 'Every man lives within ten miles of his mother-in-law.' This American man remarked:

> *I have always made it a rule that we should live in a Chinese place where there are no other relatives. Most of my wife's relatives live either in North China or in Taiwan. There are none in Hong Kong, and this has served me well. My wife would probably prefer to have relatives around, but then of course she would continually complain about them.*

The American comedian, the late George Burns, seemingly agreed, 'Happiness is having a loving, caring, close-knit family in another city!' There are cases where Chinese children move to the West to study and work and, as a result, become cosmopolitan in outlook. On returning to Asia, possibly with a Western spouse, they find their parents have not changed at all. They still do not speak any English and have no desire to embrace Western etiquette. To a westernised child, the parents could possibly be a bit of an embarrassment, especially the father. One son admitted he had never noticed it when he was young, but now it annoys him when his father is inept with knife and fork, and he shudders when his father clears his throat to spit.

In the late 1950s and 1960s, there was an exodus of Chinese men from Hong Kong, mainly from the rural New Territories, to England, where they lived and worked, and some married English women (*Mixed Marriages in the New*

Territories, 1983). Because their children have Chinese fathers, they are considered full members of the ancestral village, and they are sometimes sent back to these villages to learn the customs, the language, and how to crack melon seeds with their teeth: they must be taught to be 'real Chinese'. One can sometimes see a Eurasian wandering around a village who, when spoken to, replies with a perfect cockney or north-country English accent.

Some European wives are not exactly enamoured with Hong Kong village life and living in an old family house. They may not always appreciate the richness of the culture and the rituals; likewise, the Chinese may not fully accept European women into the community. Consequently, there have been cases where Western women have moved out in disgust, and stayed at a hotel in town. At the other extreme, one English woman who was living with her Chinese husband in a Hong Kong New Territories' village at the time of a *ta chiu* (打醮) [purification] ceremony, said, 'I have just experienced the most wonderful event of my life here in Hong Kong' (Waters, 1995:69).

There were many examples of affability between spouses and in-laws in the survey. One Chinese wife said she gets on well with her husband's family in England, genuinely enjoys visiting them, and has long telephone conversations with her mother-in-law every week. Another Chinese woman who was born and brought up in Hong Kong, and has lived in the United States for many years, wrote that all is bliss: 'My husband's parents adore me, and my parents adore him.' A Swiss wife adds:

I always got on very well with my in-laws. My mother-in-law and I were alike in many ways in spite of being from two different races. She was also a very flexible person. I also communicated very well with my Shanghainese father-in-law and worked with him sometimes. Of us three daughters-in-law, the other two are Cantonese, I was the one who was closest to him.

However, not all relationships are satisfactory. A Western man said that his Chinese mother-in-law never really accepted him, while another wrote:

My [Chinese] *wife wanted her parents to play a more active part in bringing up our children. There was even some suggestion the in-laws should move in with us. I soon scotched that. They are our kids. They don't belong to the in-laws. The relationship is now good and I think my Lo Poh (老婆) [old woman] is secretly pleased that her parents did not move in.*

In another case, back in the 1950s, the Chinese father of the bride-to-be let it be known in no uncertain terms that he did not want his daughter to marry a *gwailo*. The soon-estranged father died before the wedding took place, and the second sister's husband refused to attend the nuptials. The bride said at the reception, 'When his mother dies, I will not attend her funeral!' And she did not! In spite of everything, in the four decades since, the British husband has generally been on good terms with the remaining members of his wife's family. He has come to feel accepted, and his late mother-in-law had grown especially fond of him.

Every year at *Ching Ming* and *Chung Yeung*, this family visits the temple where the father's ashes are kept in an urn. The husband recalls clearly how, seven years after the father had died, they had all gathered at the sprawling cemetery on the slopes of a large hill one damp, chilly morning for the traditional exhumation ceremony. Two workers dug up the grave containing the sparse remains of the timber coffin, which had rotted. The father's bones were then cleaned with water and rice wine. It was important to remove all hair and any remaining flesh, as these could affect his *yang*. After the ceremony, the bones were cremated and the ashes placed in an urn in a niche in a columbarium.

> *Even as a fastidious Englishman, I do not recall anything particularly gruesome about the exhumation of my Chinese father-in-law. His bones were inert. There was no smell of death, the kind of stench that gets in your clothes and stays on your skin no matter how many times you wash. At the time, I admired the respect and filial piety shown by close members of the family to the deceased father.*

The aim of a traditional Chinese family was to have five generations under one roof, and many brides and grooms today are still wished 'a hundred sons and a thousand grandsons' (百子千孫). After all, 'if you do not sire children during the lean years, who will help you reap the harvest?' (少壯不努力，老大徒傷悲). With the prevalence of birth control (including China's one-child policy), marriages happening later in life for both men and women, the agrarian way of life disappearing in many places, not to mention urbanisation and globalisation, lifestyles are now rather different. Having five generations in one home is extremely rare anywhere in China or among the Chinese diaspora.

Other traditional beliefs and mottos include the idea that true love is like a tall, slender sugar palm, *kwong long shiu* (桄榔樹), reaching straight up to the heavens with 'one loyal heart'. Losing one's chastity was a great calamity in the old days (貞節牌坊) and the 'Four Womanly Virtues' (三從四德) were important: good character, good manners, good appearance, and good housekeeping.

Bearing children tends to patch over many problems among relatives, as this English husband wrote of his relationship with his Shanghainese in-laws:

> *We decided to get married while we were both living in England. It was another five years before we came to Hong Kong. Yes, there were problems, but not too serious. Both sets of parents were totally dismayed when we decided to get married. But they accepted the situation very quickly afterwards, and, with the birth of our son, any lingering disappointment evaporated. As we lived in England during the early years of our marriage, my wife saw more of her in-laws than vice versa. Eventually she and my father became particularly close. And when we came to Hong Kong, it was she with whom he corresponded rather than with me.*

A New Zealand husband, in turn, said that his Chinese in-laws all 'enjoy Western things like beer in the pub'. But from a different perspective, an American woman said:

> *I have a problem with my in-laws in that they don't*
> *talk to us regarding family matters that I would*
> *like to know about, such as stories about the family*
> *and anecdotes from the past. My own parents*
> *and grandparents often told us interesting things*
> *about their childhood and youth, and about their*
> *grandparents and great-grandparents. My Chinese*
> *in-laws never want to share family stories with my*
> *husband and I, or with our sons. My in-laws have*
> *lived through some interesting times and we will*
> *never learn about them.*

Oral history was also important to another Westerner, this time a British man who, over a period of half a century has tried to get his Chinese wife to 'open up'. She was a child during the Japanese occupation of Hong Kong, yet she had never really shared those experiences with him. Perhaps the memories are too unhappy? A Chinese custom that might 'help her to forget' is not to discuss the difficulties of one's family life outside the home. In the West there is, in some respects, a similar tradition. People are taught not 'to wash their dirty laundry in public'.

Whether one feels free to talk about things, negative or positive, familial or otherwise, has a bearing on the relationships within an extended family, and with the friendships one makes, and keeps. Having good friendships can make one feel secure in a new, foreign culture. Being of the minority race can make for a lonely experience.

A large number of couples in the survey said they had both Western and Chinese friends, many had about half Chinese and half Western, or of varying proportions, and sometimes those proportions changed over time and place.[8] One woman wrote that most of their friends were inter-cultural couples while other couples said most of their friends were either mainly Westerners or, totally Chinese.

'Certainly as far as I have been concerned,' a Western man said, 'marrying my Chinese wife has opened up new circles of friends for me, people who I would never have mixed with otherwise' while a Swiss woman and her Chinese husband have had long running friendships with her husband's schoolmates, all of whom have Chinese wives. Meanwhile, this American woman's response seemed to be echoed by several other spouses:

> *My friends are almost all Western women and my husband's friends are almost all Chinese men. But our 'joint' friends are generally Chinese husbands and Western wives.*

Some spouses make sure they have their own friendships, away from their partner, and hold the view that if each partner does this to some extent, a more satisfactory relationship and a stronger marriage results. One Western husband wrote that, even when his friends were Chinese and his Chinese wife's friends Westerners, they seldom mixed. A Shanghainese woman also said, 'My husband and I go our own way regarding friends, but we usually like each other's friends.' With other couples, however, if you spot one spouse outside

[8] *There are mixed marriages in Hong Kong of all kinds. In 1998, when the British Consul General held a reception at his Albany Road home, about forty cross-cultural couples of various ethnicity were invited.*

working hours, their partner is usually not far away.

Some couples mixed to a limited degree because they found they had little in common with their spouse's friends; limitations were in force both in language and in culture. Indeed, if you look around at social gatherings you will see, not infrequently, that people tend to mix and talk with people from their home country, or people of the same race. This may not be racist. I recall at the refectory in a residence hall at Manchester University in 1971-72, you could generally expect to see a table occupied entirely by Chinese. Sometimes I would go along and have my meal with them, and I was made welcome. But most of the conversation was in Cantonese and frequently they talked about 'things back home' in Singapore, Hong Kong and 'things Chinese.' It was not easy to enter fully into the discussions.

One Chinese woman made a conscious decision to avoid some of her husband's friends, due to a lack of common interests:

> *Both my husband and I have friends in*
> *common, and we also have our separate friends*
> *met through work or special group interests. For*
> *example, I am friendly with various members*
> *of an historical group whom I see socially on*
> *my own. My husband mixes with friends who*
> *play golf, ski or hike, some of whom I steer clear*
> *because they talk about their hobbies endlessly.*
> *My husband has a number of sporting interests*
> *that I don't share. I think this is so with many*
> *partners and has nothing to do with the fact that*

they are (we are) of different races.

It has been said half-jokingly that all conversation between men and women tends to be 'cross-cultural' because the two sexes can have very different interests and concerns. At some Chinese functions, men often sit together in one group and women sit in another; sometimes they are even seated at different tables for a meal.

The message came across clearly in the survey that there is always a need to be flexible and respectful, and to allow one's partner time to return to his or her native culture and friends when needed. One can picture a Chinese wife going off with friends or relatives to attend a Chinese opera when the urge takes her. The husband may find the carrying of a whip, to signify the actor is on horseback, a bit far fetched. But is this so different to when the Western husband goes off to watch football or to have a drink with the boys, neither of which may appeal to his Chinese wife? Roles can be reversed when a European husband enjoys going to Chinese temples, while the wife states that she has had her fill of that in her childhood. Then, in the West, 'hen parties' and 'birthday showers', would bore many men to tears, while at more formal, Western dinners, the ladies withdraw and leave the gentlemen to their port.

Irrespective of ethnicity, many things concerning a marital relationship boil down to personal temperament. One spouse writes:

> *My Chinese wife is socially successful and mixes*
> *equally well with Westerners and Chinese.*

*She has Western friends from Britain who still
correspond with her after twenty years. I am
less socially successful and somewhat isolated in
my home office and from my lack of Cantonese.
However, in spite of that, I get on equally well
with Chinese and Westerners.*

Other couples find themselves in similar situations. This Hong
Kong Chinese woman, who has lived in the United States for
many years, wrote:

*We have similar tastes regarding friends. The
only problem is he* [my husband] *doesn't know
how to deal with my Chinese friends who are
insufficiently westernised, and who don't speak
English well enough, so I socialise with them on
my own. But we socialise together with all his
friends and colleagues. But most of our friends are
in fact Caucasian.*

Certainly Western-Chinese friendships are viewed
differently today compared to how they were seen in the mid-
1950s. I recall a Scot saying about a Welshman, a headmaster
of a technical school, 'It's his own fault he doesn't have any
Western friends. When he first came to Hong Kong, he was far
too friendly with the Chinese.' Yet there are some Westerners,
for whatever reason, who feel more at home with Chinese
people than among their fellow Europeans.

I recall a group of young Chinese women insisting
that the Westerners they knew, bosses in their workplace,
tended to be *yam sap* (陰濕), meaning more or less 'sly',

'crafty' or liable to 'bear a grudge'. This was a remark made by women who at the time had few social contacts with Westerners. In some ways, such opinions were not unlike those of Europeans half a century ago when there was little mixing. Chinese were seen as seldom telling the truth, or only saying what you wanted to hear. Some Europeans continue to believe Chinese are 'over polite' and too helpful to friends, while sometimes rude to strangers, treating them as 'non-persons', or in other words, 'I do not know you. I can afford to ignore you.'

A few women from Europe started the 'M Club', an innovative group in the 1970s. Members were Western women married to Chinese men in Hong Kong. One member said:

> For the last thirty years, we have had a regular monthly gathering, while a smaller group of us meet more frequently for dinners in our homes and for cinema outings. We've also taken trips overseas together. A group of us Western mothers married to Chinese decided to form a club for mixed married couples and, through this, we have formed lasting friendships. Our children still keep in touch with each other, too.

The M Club has been wonderful for her. 'In the early days especially, we could share experiences and advise each other. In this way, we were able to adapt better, as well as make lasting friendships.'

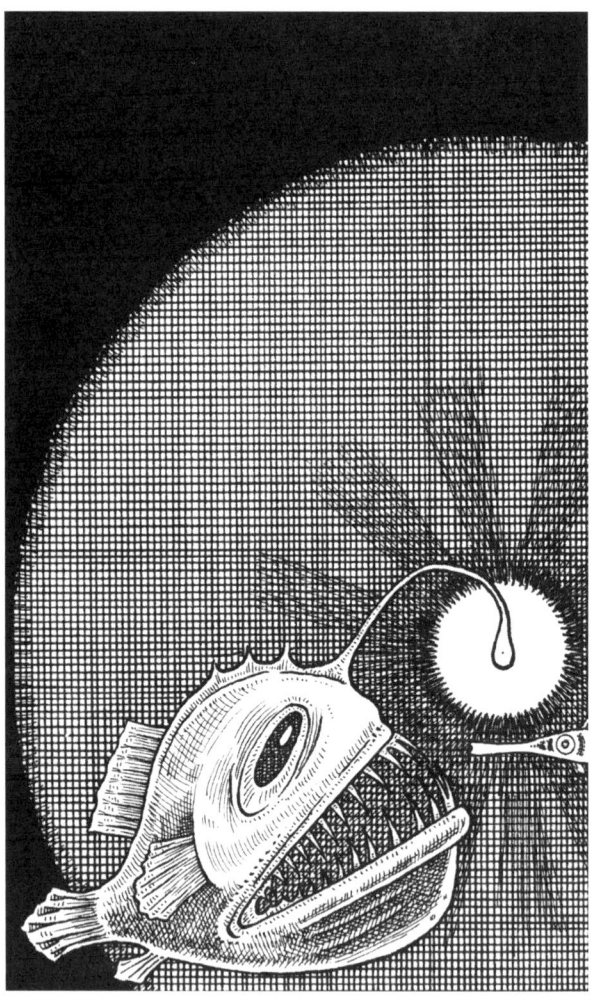

customs and habits

She does not like to kiss on the lips. 'It is very unhygienic'.

A British husband of his Hong Kong
Chinese wife

The long list of potentially irritating habits identified by our eighty-one couples include bad driving, speeding, 'the way she sidles around' to get your attention, complaining about foreign domestic helpers, the 'roving eye' and jealousy over other women, drinking with friends in the pub, bad timekeeping, lengthy discussions with waiters about ordering food in a Chinese restaurant, allowing too much time for journeys in order not to be late, and an unwillingness to accommodate a sudden change of plans with family and friends. As one wife put it, 'He would then be upset or unwilling to go to a social gathering.'

Another woman complained of her European husband walking in front of her and too fast, adding that, 'Holding hands would help!' Meanwhile, a husband complained of his wife's all consuming interest in Cantonese Opera, 'She sings it at home all the time!' Wanting to leave a function as soon as it was over annoyed another Western man, yet for many events such as wedding banquets, this is customary. The guests go early to play mahjong and chat, dinner is supposed to start at, say, eight but eventually starts at maybe nine-thirty, and as soon as the meal is over, guests promptly leave. The opening list of possibly annoying habits ends with a Chinese wife saying she was unable to appreciate fully her military historian husband's insatiable interest in dead people.

Thirty-one per cent of the respondents indicated that they believed that such annoyances would happen equally in a same-culture marriage. A Shanghainese woman wrote that when a couple first marries, they are generally on good terms and on their best behaviour. At this stage, many things intrigue, delight or amuse, and may seem exotic. Over time, a partner's habits may come to annoy, or exasperate. What a man first perceives as warmth and vulnerability in his wife-to-be, may later be seen as doormat like dependency. Some respondents were surprised, amused or annoyed by the boiling of strange, sometimes vile smelling, traditional Chinese medicine, and keeping 'nasty' herbs and odds and ends in the refrigerator; other Westerners said they partook and believed in such 'weird' brews themselves.

Social gatherings with family or friends, especially dining out at restaurants, seemed to be an area where different habits and customs come to the fore. Chinese restaurants, perhaps especially Cantonese ones, tend to be rather loud. Tables can be placed very close together, patrons and staff alike may converse in loud voices, and the layout of the establishment is often one long room with hard surfaces such as marble, mirrors and tile: all the sounds bounce loudly! The food stands as a big obstacle to enjoying and understanding Chinese people, says one New Zealand man. 'Where the food, the smell, the noise and the price all add up to something you do not enjoy, why do it? Acceptance in this area is something I have not been able to manage.' A British man felt this way:

> I find the endless wait at Chinese weddings and social occasions boring (consisting of mahjong and chatting) and I think more Western speechmaking, dancing and entertainment would be an improvement. However, there are compensations, like the casual attitude of Cantonese dinner gatherings at which guests seem to be free to arrive late, or leave the table and read a book without being considered rude. This could be classified as good or bad, so I'll call it 'amusing'.

A British man, talking about his Chinese wife whom he generally considers as 'very westernised', stated that she speaks very loudly, much louder than usual, when she is eating with her own family at a restaurant. Another Western husband agreed that westernised Chinese people often act quite differently depending on whether they are with a party of Western friends or with Chinese family members and friends. Curiously, he added that when he was the sole European among a group of Chinese, he too found himself acting differently; in some ways he was more boisterous and less inhibited, and that if he were seen by Europeans at these times, he said he would feel a little embarrassed by his own behaviour.

Problems with the culture of dining continue: several spouses were irritated by the Chinese habit of slurping. One American wife, in spite of trying hard during the course of her thirty-year marriage, has not been able to persuade her husband to stop:

> *It annoys me A LOT. He slurps all hot and even just warm beverages of food such as coffee, tea, noodles, soups, and so on. Many times I have showed him how it is possible to eat or drink liquids without slurping or making noises but he cannot be persuaded not to slurp. The slurping drives me nuts!*

A French wife also complained. In this case, however, the husband was not prepared to take it sitting down: 'I would like my wife to be more accommodating.'

A word then about slurping. To the Chinese, soup is looked upon as far more than just the ingredients. For one thing, the preparation, boiling and double boiling can go on for hours, so considerable time is invested. As soup is often prepared when someone is ill, overtired, or has just given birth, it is seen to contain care and love, too. Yet, there is another meaning behind soup: when the 'old man' was missing in the old days, a cry would go up that he had gone to the concubine's home for soup. Ah Yee Leng Tong (阿二靚湯), meaning the second wife's (the concubine's) beautiful soup, is a restaurant in Hong Kong. The name has brought a smile to many, mostly men's, faces, but by no means entirely so. My own late mother-in-law, who had had five 'mothers,' usually managed a chuckle when she recalled 'Ah Yee Leng Tong.'

Regardless, it is customary that every drop of soup be savoured and, what is more, it should be savoured hot. Slurping helps cool the precious liquid down as one imbibes; that was how it was explained to me. Slurping shows you appreciate it, I was told. An English woman puts it this way:

> *I used to (and to be truthful still do) find it annoying when he slurps soup and eats rice enthusiastically (holding the bowl to the mouth and 'scooping' rice in with chopsticks, 'rowing' rice, as the Cantonese say) and slurps soup. But slurping wasn't a problem once the children reached the age when I could explain that Daddy did not intend to be rude, and neither did Grandma when she belched at the end of a meal.*

Just as conduct acceptable in Chinese society may not be condoned among Westerners, the opposite is also true. Just as slurping annoyed Western wives, several Chinese wives disapproved of their husbands' drinking habits. One husband complained that his wife did not 'identify with having a drink before meals, especially when eating out.' One Chinese wife did not allow her husband to drink beer at home, while another wanted to make sure he did not have 'one over the eight' (After eight drinks a man gets tipsy). One woman admitted that she used to frown on her husband's drinking and believed 'it was a *gwailo* thing', but now that she herself has come to enjoy a glass of wine, she is not so disapproving.

One Western husband said that he often became annoyed with his Chinese wife's refusal to discuss problems openly, but also pointed out that he considered this to be a Chinese characteristic. The author would agree that Chinese have a tendency to speak more indirectly, to smooth things over and not upset things, and although today's young generation may be more outspoken and forthright than their elders, there is still more of an unwillingness, as a general statement, among Chinese than among Westerners not to upset the equilibrium. One Chinese woman in the survey, for instance, took part in the Hong Kong demonstrations in 1989, in which one million people protested against the Tiananmen Square incident in Beijing. She now feels that in most cases it is wrong to demonstrate, and wishes she had not taken part.

My smoothing-over and peacekeeping ways are a result of my upbringing, a Chinese woman explained:

> *My husband is more vocal in expressing his views on Chinese customs that he doesn't like. I was brought up to say things that will not trouble or inconvenience the other person.*
>
> *I am used to reading more into a given answer. For example, I will ask my husband if he wants chicken for dinner and he will answer, 'yes.' But if I ask him again, saying, 'Of course, you can have fish if you prefer that instead,' then this irritates him and*

he answers, 'You ask me again? Don't you like the first answer I gave you?'

The positive and negative sides of being appeasing were acknowledged by this man: 'My wife's loyalty, to me and colleagues, is wonderful [but] her unwillingness to 'rock the boat' can be seen as either annoying or amusing.' His wife replied that she in turn was quite irritated by her husband's tendency to take a firm and often uncompromising stance on issues which she often considered to be trivial.

A Welsh husband was seen by his wife as having a 'naive and unsophisticated honesty about expressing and displaying his feelings' while a Chinese woman who has been living in the United States for many years, had a specific comment about the people there: 'Americans are too direct and not tactful enough, boasting away in public.'

Exaggerated politeness can be a difficulty. Some Westerners have no real problem with it; in fact, some admitted that they rather like being fussed over. Yet for one English husband, this *haak hei* (客氣), the 'standing on ceremony' practice of showing extreme respect, was very hard to accept. To him, it seemed to mean, 'I am going to be so polite, that I am even going to try and prevent you from doing what you want.'

A German woman wrote that when she is dining with her in-laws, she invariably stops eating first because her appetite is smaller; her in-laws then invariably get overly concerned, thinking she does not like the food, urging her to eat more, or asking if something else is wrong. Being 'forced' to accept more food or drink can be problematic, as when most Europeans say 'yes,' they mean 'yes,' and 'no' for 'no'. Chinese, like some other Asians, the Japanese for example, are often reluctant to say 'no' and to refuse anyone.[9]

Another Chinese custom that can cause friction is bride money. Traditionally, a Chinese family considers that, on marriage, a bride leaves her natal family and joins her husband's family. To bring a girl up costs a significant sum which is often described in Cantonese as *sit boon* (蝕本) [lost profit], and the idea of 'bride money' is that the father, the traditional wage earner, is recompensed to some extent for his 'outlay.' Some Europeans whom I interviewed admitted quite openly that they had paid this 'betrothal money', while a number of bridegrooms objected to it on moral, ethical and religious grounds. 'It reduces a woman to a mere commodity' was many people's view. Interestingly, the bride herself more often than not saw it as a Chinese custom to be accepted, and that her future husband had better get used to her culture as soon as possible. One Westerner told me that when he and his wife have words and his wife says to him, 'You consider I'm worthless,' he replies, 'No you're not! You're worth HK$30,000. That's what I paid for you! Nowadays, a 'bride price' can be HK$50,000, although it must be stressed there is no hard and fast figure. Some Western grooms are 'let off' with a lesser sum, possibly HK$20,000 or HK$30,000. Others pay nothing at all, if for instance, the Chinese family is very westernised.

One Western husband summarised some cultural habits and differences in his marriage:

My wife can be a terrible timekeeper (a Chinese characteristic I believe) whilst I am the opposite, this can cause friction. I always shower in the morning, which she did not like, while she showered at night: now we both shower morning and nights! She doesn't mind loud conversation and noise, whereas I am the opposite; I prefer soft lights, particularly when eating, whilst she likes to see everything in full glare. I believe these are in the main cultural, rather than personal differences.

This respondent was not the only person to mention the habit many Chinese have of taking a bath at night while Westerners typically prefer to bathe in the morning. Of course, bathing twice a day is not unusual in the tropics. Other Chinese thought it strange that their Western husbands liked to sleep in their birthday suits!

Other habits that seemed rather strange to the average Westerner included using a tongue scraper first thing in the morning to remove 'fur' when one brushes one's teeth, and using a damp towel to 'dry' oneself after washing one's face.[10] Shortly after meeting her future husband, one Chinese woman was surprised (and a trifle shocked) when he blew his nose with gusto (much louder than a Chinese would). A little later, two more puzzles: he washed his face directly with lather from soap on his hands instead of using a face cloth, and made weird noises when gargling. 'I wondered what on

10 *Such customs today are mainly followed by older Chinese people.*

earth you were doing,' she told him years later. Meanwhile, an Englishman said that the Chinese way of drinking and retaining liquid in one's mouth before swallowing it, really is effective and refreshing especially in hot weather.

Certainly hygiene is considered very important in Chinese culture, especially perhaps in regions which can be very humid and subtropical, and where disease can spread quickly. There is a particular concern that germs may enter the body via the various orifices: eyes, ears, nostrils, mouth, anus and urinary tract. Babies, for instance, are often more nuzzled than kissed, because of the risks of passing germs. One European husband, who was getting on in years, was surprised when his Chinese wife of long standing suddenly told him she did not like to kiss on the lips anymore. 'It is very unhygienic,' she explained. The European accepted this as it did seem sensible, but he was still a little hurt. A Dutchman, however, who attended a conference in Hong Kong in the mid-1960s maintained that the most important thing he learned during his one-week stay was that Chinese women do kiss!

A Welsh husband in the survey categorised the characteristics of his Chinese wife under three sub-headings:

> ***Amusing**: her disinclination to get wet when it's raining (as if she is afraid she will dissolve); **endearing**: her assumption about the superiority of Chinese culture; and **irritating**: her willingness (sometimes approaching determination) to permit telephone calls to or from her friends and family to last inordinately*

long times, frequently more than half an hour.

'Long' telephone conversations annoyed other couples in the survey, too. Some said calls lasted considerably longer than half an hour.

Another area of difference is filial piety. Westerners seldom view this in quite the same way as Chinese do. Several feel uncomfortable about supporting one's parents on a regular basis, as is the custom for many Chinese adult children, especially the sons, but often for adult daughters, too. One Western woman confided:

> *Even when we were living in* [Mainland] *China and earning very low salaries, with no savings, money had to be sent to his parents. I'd never met them, and they had never welcomed me into their home because I was older than him, and didn't intend to have children. They thought I would take their son overseas, eventually. I was a 'non-person' to them.*

In several cases, it was agreed before marriage that a couple would support the Chinese parents, and one Chinese wife supported her widowed mother out of her own salary. With little in the way of social security, most Chinese people accept readily that parents must be provided for in old age.

One English husband, a man accustomed to keeping a stiff upper lip, had many observations to make on the night of his mother-in-law's death, a night he vividly recalls:

> *My wife and her two sisters, with no prearranged*

signal, burst into exaggerated, high-pitched wailing around the body. I appreciated their grief was real and they felt this was the proper way to express themselves on the occasion, although I felt unable to do likewise. After a period, the wailing stopped just as abruptly as it had started, and the situation came under control. The wailing had summoned the gods, and they were thus able to carry out their duties.

The husband was somewhat surprised at his wife's behaviour by the death bed, because she was a Catholic, although not particularly fervent. In some ways, he was glad she wailed as she did. He did not want his wife to be too westernised, although other Westerners might have seen the sudden expression of emotion around the mother's body as being too extreme, insincere, or even 'distasteful.' The event illustrated clearly to him that, underneath it all, his wife was at heart very Chinese; he also knew that the wailing was an important start to the long, complex process of grieving – much more complex than with a Western funeral. With cross-cultural marriages, there are frequently differences in the ways spouses handle crises, such as a death. Some cultures believe pain should be handled stoically, as the British are taught, while in other cultures, it is expected that people will vent their feelings outwardly, such as by wailing, or even singing and dancing.

Perhaps because Chinese culture is so much older than European cultures for example, Chinese people may have more of a tendency to summarise the 'way things are done.'

This English husband said:

> I was amused when early in our relationship my
> wife would say such things as 'We Chinese do this,
> that or the other,' as if speaking on behalf of 1.2
> billion of them. She in turn was surprised that I
> could not tell her what 'we English do.' All I could
> tell her was what I myself do or whatever, without
> promising to speak on behalf of all my fellow
> countrymen.

His wife put one example forward:

> Ways to care for loved ones are different. Chinese ask
> frequently about the well-being of the other person,
> everything from the simple state of comfort to details
> of a pain or illness.

Chinese people do ask frequently about the well-being
of another person, I agree. I seem to have picked up the habit!
When I was in England on leave in the early 1970s, I said to a
Welshman with some concern in my voice, 'Where have you
been? I haven't seen you for a long time!' His straight to the
point reply was: 'What is it to do with you where I've been?'
I then began to realise that, having lived in Hong Kong for
several years, I must be more tactful when communicating
with fellow British acquaintances, particularly when asking
about their well-being. In fact, such incidents lead Chinese
to claim that Europeans are *siu hei* (小氣) [small air, meaning
overly sensitive or narrow-minded] or *yam saap* (陰濕)
[underhanded].

Another British husband stated in his questionnaire that gift giving can cause problems. While it might be said Chinese people, as is often said about many Asian peoples, can be more generous than Westerners, one could also ask, 'When does the giving of presents end and corruption begin?' Corruption is rife in Mainland China, and was in Hong Kong until the Independent Commission Against Corruption was established in 1974. Judging by Asian standards, Hong Kong today is a fairly 'clean' society.

Giving gifts within the family can create another set of much lesser 'problems'. Unlike the Chinese, many Westerners do not like to give money; they prefer personally selected gifts, often quoting the expression, 'It's the thought that counts.' Chinese people, however, have a long tradition of giving 'lucky money' – *lai see* (利是), particularly at the Lunar New Year, easily the most festive holiday of the year comparable in scale to Christmas or Hanukkah in other cultures. Crisp, clean bank notes are neatly folded and inserted into small red envelopes and presented politely, with both hands, to various family members. School children will be wished, for example, 'Step, step, high promote' (步步高昇) in a rhyming tone. In return, the elderly will be wished may you be 'As healthy as a dragon or a horse' (龍馬精神) and so on. This act of giving reinforces the roles within a family: people know and feel that they belong. Married couples also distribute New Year *lai see* to friends' children, acquaintances, colleagues, friends who are 'unmarried', and even to an 'old maid' of sixty or more. The amount of 'lucky money' that changes hands can be staggering.

One European husband in the survey wrote he was surprised that, on receiving a present, he was supposed to return the generosity by giving a *lai see* envelope containing a small amount of money 'to return the luck.' Although not as common as it used to be, this Chinese custom is typically only followed by elderly people now, and then usually at the New Year or on birthdays. Another British man compared how his mother in England always insisted that, if a knife or a pair of scissors (anything that could 'cut' friendship) was given as a present, one must give that person in return a coin, no matter how small.

living east, living west

I have given up thinking about where I belong: part of
me is European and part of me is Asian.

A Eurasian youngster

Spouses in Western-Chinese marriages have a choice.
They can resist their spouse's culture and continue to think
and lead their lives as they always have. Conversely, they can
submerge themselves in their partner's culture and, to a certain
extent, reject their own. Or, they can blend the two cultures.
Most couples in this survey – whether they live in Asia or
the West – seem to live in a mixture of lifestyles and cultures,
although many followed mainly Western ways. The general
consensus was that living in a cosmopolitan city was the easiest
way to get the best of both the Chinese and Western worlds,
and to secure their children exposure to both heritages.

Religion can be a foundation of a lifestyle. Looking at
people's faiths, around thirty-eight per cent of the respondents
identified themselves as Protestants, about twenty-two per
cent as Roman Catholics, and some said they had lapsed and
were 'sort of Christians'.■ There were about the same number

■ In 'Hong Kong English' and in some other Chinese
communities, the term 'Christian' is often used
incorrectly to mean a 'Protestant'. This is purely
custom over many years, albeit incorrect. So, people
in Hong Kong will say, 'He is not a Christian, he
is a Catholic.'

of Christians among Chinese and Western spouses, with one British man keen to point out that he was a Christian complete with tambourine! About twenty-five percent left the space blank or wrote that they did not believe in any doctrine, with one couple saying that 'organised religions today all seem hypocritical and cause more problems, wars and intolerance than most other factors in the world.' Buddhists comprised about seven per cent of our sample, a few of whom were fervent, while a number said they also followed certain aspects of Chinese folk religion. This includes Taoism, (the only religion indigenous to China), animism (whereby spirits are thought to live in animate and inanimate things, commonly trees and rocks), and *feng shui* (風水) [the practice of aligning environmental currents and cosmic principles in homes, offices, graves and other places].

One Chinese husband believed that 'having the same religious faith is essential for a successful marriage' and indeed, Parseeism, Judaism and Catholicism, do not permit or have strict rules about marrying outside the faith. Some religions insist that all paths lead to the same God, and in some of the households in our survey, different religions were practised within the same family. Harmony can be maintained, but sometimes friction can occur, as one Christian spouse writes:

> *On arriving home after work, I'm greeted by Buddhist chanting and incense smoke. It's so upsetting.*

A Catholic was more flexible. Each year, the Briton concerned wore a different animal pendant from the Chinese zodiac around his neck, as requested by his wife. 'It didn't do any harm', he said. 'It might even do a bit of good!'

The survey indicates that quite a number of seemingly fervent European Christians dabble in Chinese folk religion and superstitions which, as far as the Church is concerned, could be taboo. Interestingly, some churches in Chinese communities have accepted certain Chinese customs, a flexibility appreciated by many Chinese people. At a Catholic funeral in Hong Kong, for example, people normally bow three times to the dead person's large photograph followed by another bow to the immediate family mourners. Curiously and conveniently, many things are in three's in both Christianity and Taoism. The Holy Trinity, for instance, aligns with three major Taoist gods: *Fuk* (福) [Blessings], *Luk* (祿) [Prestige] and *Sow* (壽) [Longevity], and in some respects is similar to *Tin, Dei, Yan* (天，地，人) [Heaven, Earth and Mankind], which crops up frequently in folk religion, where often one joss stick is burned for each of the three parts of the universe.[12]

Certainly, a number of spouses believe in hedging their bets and, as one British Christian husband said, 'Yes to *Ching Ming*, yes to *feng shui*, yes to all festivals!' Another 'atheist but tolerant' Briton and his not particularly active Christian Chinese wife say grace with the kids to keep them broad minded. As a whole, the family follows both Chinese and Christian festivals but 'without great spiritual commitment'. Similar views were held by several other couples. As one British father said, the family is happy to sing Christmas carols and 'for years we swept graves with the in-laws, but now we have

[12] In complex Chinese culture, there are also the 'Four Womanly Virtues' (good character, good manners, good appearance and good housekeeping) and the 'Four Vices' (women, gambling, drinking and smoking). Then there are the 'Five Elements' (Fire, Water, Wood, Metal and Earth) which are important in fortune telling, and the 'Five Personal Relationships' (Ruler and Subject, Husband and Wife, Father and Son, Elder and Younger Brothers, and Friend and Friend).

lapsed, although the wife may still sometimes go alone.' He added, 'She has no attachment to *feng shui,* although she may align the elephant statue to keep the devils at bay, and so on, but not seriously.'

In *feng shui,* wind and water, harmony and balance are two important goals. Items in buildings, graves, the work-place and so on, must be designed and positioned so that they 'reconcile' with environmental currents and cosmic principles. Fortune plants (*Fu Kwai Chuk*) (富貴竹) and small crystal containers containing salt water, to absorb impurities in the atmosphere and other objects are strategically placed in the home. Lucky colours, numbers and charms are also important, especially among the Cantonese as opposed to the Shanghainese. For example, *feng shui* can be an expensive 'religion' to follow, as *feng shui* masters are frequently called in to provide expert, and expensive, advice. *Feng shui* has become popular in the West, as indicated by the increasing number of English-language publications on the subject in recent years.

One Chinese wife regularly consults the *Tung Sing* (通勝) for the 'good' and 'bad' days on which to carry out certain activities, while a very westernised Chinese husband in the survey never travels without checking the 'know-all book' (Windridge, 1999); this used to annoy his wife, but now she accepts it. The original name for *Tung Sing* was *Tung Shue* (通書) meaning 'general book', sometimes described as the 'Know-all-Book.' But, as the character for book, *shue* (書), sounds similar to the character for 'lose', people created a more auspicious title: *Tung Sing* [generally win].

Probably pre-dating 2205 BC, the *Tung Sing* is thought to be the world's oldest continuous publication and is largely unchanged since its original printed edition in the fifth-century. The annual is a bestseller in Chinese communities; almost one million copies are sold every year in Hong Kong alone.

The *Tung Sing*, based on the Lunar Calendar, includes comprehensive information on subjects like *feng shui* and palmistry, but much of the book is about date-choosing. It is important not to upset their people or gods when selecting days for tasks such as changing the goldfish water or 'crossing a river by boat', which might refer to taking Hong Kong's popular Star Ferry across the harbour. Even more personal matters are mentioned: 'Not tonight, dear, it's not propitious!' Certainly sexual intercourse does not take place when a family is in mourning, or during the time of a village *ta chiu*, a purification festival. After one couple in the survey had selected their wedding day, in 1960, the Chinese mother-in-law took the precaution of checking the *Tung Sing*. Fortunately, it was a lucky day and everyone was happy. As the groom said at the time, 'If it makes her happy, why not?'

In money-oriented Chinese society, considerable attention is paid to the *Tung Sing* for conducting business, too. Chinese business people, well known for their flexibility, find a way to get around what can be many cumbersome restrictions found in the *Tung Sing*. While some Chinese business people do not disclose to Westerners that they consult the *Tung Sing* in their corporate lives, English language versions of the book have also been published, and re-published. In fact, the book can be compared to *Old Moore's Almanac* in England, which one European husband in the survey recalls his mother always kept behind a vase on the mantel. Over in North America, too, *The Old Farmer's Almanac* claims to be the oldest continuously published periodical. The original Robert B. Thomas *Farmer's Almanac* was founded in 1792. Today's younger generations seem to be using the *Tung Sing* and its international equivalents less and less, although many people change as they grow older and sometimes, in Hong Kong in particular, become more superstitious.

This happened twice in a Hong Kong Chinese woman's family in our survey, in two generations. As a teenager at a Catholic secondary school, she got baptized, confirmed, became a strong Catholic, and to her great satisfaction, persuaded her mother to convert, too. After a few years, without saying why, her mother stopped going to Mass and started following Chinese folk religion, such as burning joss sticks at the family altar. Meanwhile the daughter, now in her late teens, met a European Anglican, whom she also convinced to convert. They had a Catholic wedding, attended mass on Holy Days of Obligation, abstained from meat on Fridays and led a life of the Church. Then in the 1980s, she, like her mother earlier, switched to popular religion, especially *feng shui* and 'ancestral worship'.[13]

The Catholic husband, who now attends Mass alone, believes that family unity is important, and they pay respects together at relatives' graves on the two main days for the dead:

13 Not all religions agree with the term 'ancestor worship', and prefer the term 'ancestor reverence'. They maintain one should only worship the Supreme Being.

Ching Ming (清明) (sometimes called the Chinese Easter) and *Chung Yeung* (重陽) [Double Ninth, or the ninth day of the ninth month in the lunar calendar]. In fact, when the husband was a child in rural England, he liked putting flowers on the family graves in the churchyard. In the company of his older relatives, he learned about his forebears, about his roots, and has never forgotten. He sees it as being similar to the way Chinese people visit ancestral graves and respect deceased relatives.

The Chinese believe that the gravesite must be carefully chosen, and good *feng shui* is imperative, including the direction a grave is facing. A good site depends on the lie of the land, on 'good sight lines', preferably overlooking water, and other factors. The Chinese might compare the grave to an 'antenna' that 'connects' the living with the dead; the better the grave and its surroundings, and the more the deceased is worshipped, the more the living members of the family will be protected and blessed. Visiting the grave can take on an air of a family gathering, even a picnic. A suckling pig, crisp and golden-brown, food for the ancestors and the gods, is typically offered up, and afterwards, the family eats the delicious pork, sometimes right at the gravesite.

Returning to the same couple, this wife strongly objected to her husband wanting to donate his organs on death and wanting to scatter his cremated ashes on Hong Kong's Victoria Peak. 'How would we be able to visit you at *Ching Ming?*' She believes the Chinese saying, 'Thou should not inflict harm on one's body, not even hair and skin because they were inherited from one's parents (身體髮膚受之父母).' In Hong Kong, up to the 1950s, if a person had an operation and then died, relatives might request that the removed body parts be buried with the corpse; the body should be complete, ready for reincarnation. The husband understood that one person's superstition is another's religion, and dropped his proposals.

Other families in our survey follow both Chinese and Western customs. One American wife with a Chinese husband wrote:

> Our children are now grown up and living on their own in the United States. However, when they were in Hong Kong, we did everything. We celebrated all Christian holidays, and most American ones like Independence Day, as well. We also did all Chinese things, such as, kowtowing, pouring tea for my husband's grandparents on their birthdays and Chinese New Year, visiting graves at Ching Ming, buying lanterns at Mid-Autumn Festival, eating moon cakes, going to 'bai neen' (拜年) [visiting relatives and friends] at Chinese New Year. I myself, although an American, take feng shui very seriously, but no one else in the family does now. I have also been very interested in Chinese medicine, acupuncture and tai chi (太極). But I am the only one in the family who seems, really, to care about these things.

There are several cases where, interestingly, roles were reversed and the Western spouse follows Chinese customs more readily than the Chinese partner. It seemed more common for the Western wife to be the one to make sure that the Eurasian children be well versed in both heritages, particularly Chinese customs. One Australian woman wrote that her Chinese husband leads an easy going, informal Western lifestyle:

> *I have adopted and follow Chinese customs more so than does my husband who is happy as long as he can play tennis and golf, and have relaxation time with the family. Our three, now grown-up children are very Chinese and are very interested in feng shui, Buddhism and our Chinese family history.*

There were also many couples who said they led largely Western lifestyles. This is not difficult to do in 'East meets West' places like Singapore or Hong Kong where several couples said their lives were very westernised although they followed or believed in certain Chinese customs or principles, such as showing particular respect to the elderly. Many of these couples acknowledge the major holidays, such as Chinese New Year. One such Chinese wife had a keen interest in *feng shui* and 'put various things, for good luck, around the house', including the 'fortune plant'. Otherwise, 'We lead a normal, Western, urban lifestyle.'

In fact, a large number of the respondents said they pay regard to both Chinese and Western traditions, customs and activities, such as the Lunar New Year, the Lantern Festival, Christmas, *Ching Ming* and *Chung Yeung*. Many also attend regular Chinese family gatherings, and most Western spouses encourage their partners not to forget their Chinese heritage.

'When you drink the water remember the source' (飲水思源).
Many spouses said that their Eurasian children enjoy receiving
red *lai see* packets (of course they do!) and eating *dim sum*
(點心), meaning 'touch the heart', a common Cantonese-style
breakfast, brunch or lunch, especially popular on Sundays. One
spouse insisted that the family dabbles in *feng shui* but only for
fun.

As one would expect, among the respondents, the
Chinese spouse is usually more serious about Chinese customs
than his or her Western partner, but this is by no means always
so. Some Westerners are extremely interested. One Chinese
wife wrote:

> *Only I visit my family graves from time to time; my*
> *European husband never does. We seldom talk about*
> *feng shui. I think our lifestyle is quite westernised.*

Several times, Westerners in the survey were criticised for not
supporting their Chinese wives, such as by going off on a boat
trip with their pals and crates of beer at Lunar New Year; the
men explained their behaviour by claiming they did not 'fit in'
and only 'got in the way'. One New Zealand husband wrote
that he respects all Chinese customs but does not live by them.
'I [do] participate in all functions where my wife requests my
presence.'

'Traditions' or 'superstitions', depending on one's
perspective, can play a large part in a Western-Chinese
marriage, especially with a Hong Kong-raised spouse,
and especially if the couple resides in Hong Kong. Several

questionnaires indicate, for instance, that the Shanghainese generally do not follow Chinese traditions as strictly as the Cantonese. In Mainland China, which experienced several purges of 'down with the old', discouraged or outlawed certain 'feudal' customs, in Hong Kong, many traditions, or superstitions, can be very much alive. Earth gods' shrine dot the fronts of houses and shops. Incense coils hang at many a temple. The *Tung Sing* is for sale at many stationery shops.

One Hong Kong couple wrote that interaction with the wife's Chinese family included many elements of Chinese lifestyle such as observance of Lunar New Year, eating mooncakes, attending lantern festivals, and polishing the bones of their ancestors at *Ching Ming* and *Chung Yeung*. In Hong Kong, there are various ossuaries where bones are stored, and at the two festival times, some families reverently take the bones out of the niches or urns or wherever they are stored, and spread the bones out under the sun to improve the *feng shui* of the family.

One English architect said:

> My Chinese wife can be very 'Cantonese superstitious'
> which can be frustrating and difficult to understand
> at times. But I have got used to it. She follows all
> Cantonese traditions and superstitions, so, yes, we
> pay regard to feng shui, festivals and temple visits.
> Conversely we also live, in parallel, what might be
> described as a very international lifestyle.

One Caucasian husband said that his wife talks about *feng shui* a lot and believes in 'portents and some superstitions'. In turn, a British husband mentioned the following 'taboos' in Hong Kong society:

> *My* [Hong Kong] *wife does not like me to wear my favourite, green, sports cap as this signifies she has a boy friend and thereby embarrasses her among friends, relatives and neighbours. I once took a book to read when accompanying my wife to a mahjong party. She was angry because in Cantonese the word for 'book'* (書) *sounds similar to the word for 'lose'* (輸)*, implying she would lose at mahjong.*

He continued that you also must not tease or joke with someone when they are playing mahjong. This might also make them lose.

To be fair, it is not, of course, just the Chinese who have such sayings. Many Westerners think twice about walking under ladders and have a spook if a Friday falls on the thirteenth of the month. One respondent recalled how his English mother would not allow finger and toe nails to be cut on a Sunday in case 'one had the devil with one all the week'.

One family living in Hong Kong visits the monastery where the ashes of relatives are kept, pays attention to *feng shui* and *Tung Sing*, and makes an annual visit to the Wong Tai Sin Temple in Hong Kong, the last of which can be a taxing activity for all concerned because of the massive crowds. The family also travels to Bangkok every year to pray at the 'Four-Faced Buddha'. A Chinese woman added:

Yes, we visit my father's grave at Ching Ming and pay regard to feng shui even if it does mean putting a clock in an awkward position so one has to crane one's neck around to see the time. Basically, we observe each other's cultural differences without really examining the reasons. They are just accepted.

Sir Jimmy McGregor was quoted in *M Magazine* as being largely a 'Chinese in a *gwailo* body' (King, C., 1996:8). He said he believes in old-fashioned Chinese principles and liked the idea of the extended family system as a unit. 'It's almost like a soap opera at times with our family members scattered around the globe. You should hear the stories that come up when sitting at the dinner table!' Jimmy McGregor and his family moved to Vancouver to live in 1997, the year of the return of Hong Kong, and one wonders to what extent they lead a Chinese lifestyle now.

For couples living anywhere in the West, it is generally harder to observe Chinese festivals, which are primarily based on either the lunar or solar calendar, [14] and may thus fall on ordinary working days. Yet many larger cities around the world have Chinese community centres of sorts that hold various functions. One active group in England is the 'Friends' of the Royal Asiatic Society Hong Kong Branch, which holds a Chinese New Year lunch in London every year, always a very lively gathering with plenty of chatter and noise in true Hong Kong style.

'Where possible we follow Chinese customs, plus Christmas,' a couple who now lives in England wrote. In

[14] For example, Chinese New Year and Chung Yeung are based on the Lunar calendar. Ching Ming usually falls on 5 April and the Winter Solstice falls on the shortest day of the year.

another instance, a Chinese woman, who was born and
brought up in Hong Kong, wrote that she and her United
States born Caucasian husband tend to follow American
customs: 'Not too much in the way of Chinese customs.
We may have a Chinese meal at Lunar New Year, but that's
about it.' A British husband living in Hong Kong puts it this way:

> *We do enough to keep the relatives happy. We visit*
> *graves at Ching Ming in Hong Kong and go to*
> *Church at Christmas if we happen to be in Britain*
> *at that time of year. This is not out of conviction,*
> *but for an easy life. We celebrate Christmas,*
> *although neither my wife nor I are religious. We do*
> *this because our son likes us all to be together as a*
> *family at this time.*

His Chinese wife continued:

> *My parents were buried in England and I visit*
> *their graves from time to time (not necessarily at*
> *Ching Ming), either by myself or with siblings*
> *if they happen to be there at the time. My*
> *husband and I are not particularly traditional.*
> *My Chinese parents were themselves highly*
> *westernised and did not go in for Chinese*
> *superstitious, customs and beliefs. I think it is*
> *almost impossible these days, certainly in a place*
> *like Hong Kong, to follow a completely Chinese*
> *lifestyle. With globalisation, cultural differences*
> *have become blurred. There is less pressure on*
> *mixed marriages as a result, because there is less*
> *conflict in the choice of lifestyles, as Hong Kong's*

*middle and professional classes increasingly
pursue Western ways and thoughts. This trend
is spreading to the Chinese Mainland and can
clearly be seen in places like Shanghai and
Beijing.*

In her book, *Foreign Devils*, published in 2002, May
Holdsworth expresses a similar view, especially regarding
Eurasian children: 'Hong Kong's educated class inhabits a
sort of hybrid cultural zone, more westernised than strictly
Chinese.' 'After World War Two,' she said, 'Hong Kong
Eurasians have adapted well,' as this youngster seems to
confirm:

> *I feel Eurasian. I do not feel totally European or
> Chinese. I have given up thinking about where
> I belong: part of me is European and part of me
> is Asian. It is a tremendous advantage because I
> feel I can bridge the gap between the two cultures
> (Hughes, 1994:19).*

On the other hand this teenager says he is more comfortable
living in Asia. 'It's more difficult for us in Europe. It's not really
home [there].'

Again and again, the merging of two worlds comes
across. Certainly if you were to walk into my Hong Kong
home you would be able to tell straight away that it's not an
ordinary British household. First, there are 'fortune plants', a
variety of crystal ornaments, and several dishes, each containing
one antique silver and six antique bronze coins placed in
strategic *feng shui* positions around the flat. The figurines and

pictures include the Chinese Goddess of Mercy, the Chinese God of Longevity and the Athenian Philosopher, Socrates, among others. I could go on. The contents of my home fairly accurately mirror our cross-cultural lifestyle, as homes of other couples in the survey might also very well indicate.

'Do you believe it is easier for a Western-Chinese marriage to be happier within a Chinese community, in a place like Singapore, Taiwan or Hong Kong, as opposed to living in a Western environment?' was another question posed to the eighty-one couples. Although not every couple had lived both in the East and the West, and could not comfortably compare the two experiences, most had good ideas on where they stood.

One British husband, a retired police officer, came straight to the point, 'My wife has visited Britain and she doesn't like it! She would never consider living anywhere other than in Hong Kong.'

Another husband took a similar view. 'Of course, it's easier for my Chinese wife to live in Hong Kong. She has the support of her family and friends here.' Another Chinese wife felt much the same. Although her views have changed somewhat over the years, she now admits she could be happy in a place like Singapore or Hawaii, both of which have large Chinese communities. While many Chinese do appreciate the peaceful atmosphere of countries like Canada, with its lack of stress, others prefer the 'get-up-and-go' spirit of Hong Kong which never seems to sleep. One Shanghainese wife complained that her European husband took her back to 'sleepy' Luxembourg to live where it was decidedly 'love in a cold climate'. They managed for six months before returning to Taiwan, because they both missed the *yit naau* (熱鬧) [hot and scold], an expression which can translate as 'bustling', 'hurly-burly' or 'exciting'.

A large number of respondents felt much the same way. It is easier for a Western-Chinese couple to be happy living within a predominantly Chinese community rather than in the West. After all, places like Singapore, Hong Kong and Taipei are international, with a good standard of living and a high life expectancy, and with strong Western and Chinese influences. Many middle-class Westerners and Asians of different nationalities live together in the same apartment buildings, and they may join the same clubs. In addition, both Singapore and Hong Kong use English and Chinese as official languages. One couple said that they had spent all their married life in Hong Kong, living in what they saw as basically a Chinese city with a Western veneer.

A French woman and her Chinese husband said that they started off their married life in England, then, after twelve years, as more mature adults, they moved to Hong Kong, where they felt it was easier to live. Totally opposite are a Chinese husband and his German wife; they complained of some English wives in Hong Kong being snobbish, and prefer a third country in the West, like England. One spouse shares the following views:

> *It varies. I think it is possibly easier for the*

*Chinese person in the relationship to be happier
in Hong Kong. On the other hand it is easier for
the Western person to be happier in a Western
country. We have many mixed-marriage friends.
The husbands are usually Chinese. The wives are
usually Western (American, British, Australian
or European). The husbands all love Hong Kong
and want to stay here. Most of the wives love
Hong Kong too, but it is a 'love-hate' relationship
and European wives usually need to get out of
cramped Hong Kong sometime and go back
[home] for their 'cultural fix'.*

Other interviewees say that when they return to their
hometown, they often feel disoriented and miss Hong Kong's
little things, like the outlying islands and the Earth God
shrines. 'America is so 'un-spiritual' and the culture seems
somewhat contrived, even its air of being developed,' an
American wife wrote (McCord, 2000). It is appreciated that
Western countries differ considerably, even within the United
States, or Britain:

*So much varies depending on where you live
in the West. In Britain, by chance, I have only
lived in ethnically diverse places. I was born in
Leicester which has fifty-five per cent Indian and
a large eastern European population. I studied
in central London, taught in Bradford which has
a forty per cent Pakistani population and later
lived in Chinatown in Edinburgh.*

It was in the main agreed by respondents that a couple

could probably settle better in a large cosmopolitan city, as opposed to a closely-knit village or town. Even though so much has changed over recent years, and a number of Chinese restaurants and take-aways dot towns in countries like England, acceptance into a small community is still seen as being more difficult. With an increase in immigration, both legal and illegal, some communities in England, and elsewhere, can be less tolerant of outsiders.

One Chinese husband with an English wife said, straightforwardly, 'No,' he did not think they would be happier living in a Chinese city like Singapore or Hong Kong. Another Chinese man also came straight to the point: 'It is easier in the West.' These two 'take-it-or-leave-it' views were tempered by an Australian woman who said that it may have been true in the 1970s and 1980s, but now it is different:

> I am the Western member of the family, but wherever we travel, and within the circle in which we mix, whichever country or state, the Chinese community is a well established group of people.

There are those who believe that because the West is more multi-cultural, differences are more readily accepted. One Chinese wife sees many advantages there:

> I think we would be happier in Canada, specifically Toronto, because my family is there. The space, air, easy access to fresh food and laid-back lifestyle are better, too. But Hong Kong does provide things we cannot do in Canada, the chance to travel easily within Asia, and jobs that

pay well, for a start.

Living in Hong Kong was not good for a New Zealand woman and her Mainland Chinese now ex-husband:

> *He hated Hong Kong. I have a strong feeling we got on better in New Zealand.*

One Englishman cautioned not to generalise, that cross-cultural marriages fail regularly, both in Chinese cities and elsewhere. He did add that a couple which starts out living in a Chinese city and then moves elsewhere has challenges to face. On the whole, he thought his wife preferred living in Hong Kong because it is more 'familiar'. Another English husband wrote:

> *A mixed marriage requires cultural adaptability from its partners that will often be greater for one than for the other. This could influence both the choice of lifestyle and place of residence. Choosing Singapore or Hong Kong could make life easier if the Chinese partner was less adaptable because of, say, language limitations. On the other hand, we know several mixed couples where the Chinese wives say they would prefer to live in England rather than in Hong Kong.*

In turn, his Chinese wife wrote:

> *I do not know anyone who lives in a purely Chinese community as such. We all try to find our own 'comfort zones' in which inevitably lives crisscross. Generally, we interact with people with*

whom we have interests in common, and in my
case, these people are both Chinese and Western.
I would never choose to live in one community
rather than the other. Why should one restrict
oneself unnecessarily? Having said that, there
are perhaps advantages in Hong Kong that can
help to reduce tension in marriage. For example,
young mothers are less tied and stressed when
there is domestic and babysitting assistance… It
is in the area of tedious household chores that the
limit of my cultural adaptability kicks in!

An Englishman said that he found Chinese people to
be more 'open-minded' toward cross-cultural marriage and
felt that the English 'can be quietly very prejudiced in their
views,' An American said that acceptance by mainstream
Chinese society probably depends more on the social class and
occupations of the couple, and if the non-Chinese partner
learns to speak Chinese and interacts easily with the local
population. Nevertheless, he said, there is probably a numbers
threshold; as long as numbers are relatively small, vis-a-vis
the majority, all would be fine. He and his Chinese wife,
both academics, lived in New York City for a short period
before moving to Hong Kong. In an academic environment
anywhere, he says, a cross-cultural marriage is not an unusual
phenomenon. He firmly believes that his wife would not be
happy in the United States, anywhere. Even though Hong
Kong is not 'her China' (she is from the north), it has, the
husband said, provided a very culturally comfortable place to
live, work and raise a family.

But then, with different views again, a Welshman insisted:

In our own case I don't think the domicile makes much, if any, difference. We are very happy when we are in England (usually for about three months in every year) or when visiting places such as Perth [Australia], *to visit my wife's mother, or Cebu in the Philippines where we have a condominium.*

One Chinese wife, originally from Malaysia but who has lived in England for several years said, in her own words of wisdom, 'It doesn't matter where the couple live; if they're happy within themselves and with each other, they can live anywhere.'

Does this statement also apply for one's place of retirement? Does deciding where to work and raise one's family have different considerations from choosing where to wind one's life down? In our survey, about 28 per cent said they had already retired, and a number had chosen Hong Kong as their last place of residence.

In the nineteenth and early twentieth centuries, Hong Kong was not a healthy place. Typhoid and tuberculosis were common, and a preponderance of rats carried many diseases through overcrowded tenements, helped by a very humid climate. Only a few Old Hong Kong Hands would retire there, one of the first being Hector MacLean, who died in Hong Kong in 1894 at the age of fifty-seven. MacLean worked for Jardines and fathered Sir Robert Ho Tung's first wife, Lady Margaret. His remains lie in a special section of the old Colonial Cemetery in Happy Valley, now called the Hong Kong Cemetery, an area reserved for residents who had lived in Hong Kong for over twenty years. At the end of World War Two, there were still just a few expatriate retirees, and since then, there has been a gradual increase. Today, a number of us stay on.

One Hong Kong Chinese woman who married just after World War Two settled in England with her British husband. They both wanted their children to be brought up either in England or in China, rather than in a place with a mixed culture like colonial Hong Kong. Although her husband died years ago, she remains in England, now retired, and has a great affection for the country, where she said she has never experienced racism.

When I was on Special Constable Police duty during the 1956 riots in Hong Kong, I recall my commanding officer telling me that he was going home to Scotland to retire in six weeks time. 'I want to see the four seasons again,' a smile creased his face. He was dead within eighteen months. After a full working life in Asia, it could have been that the change was too much for him to bear in advancing years. Also, going back to one's birth place and retracing one's steps is never easy, whether one has a Chinese wife or not. The place has always changed, the air has lost its invigorating qualities, and at the same time, one has evolved and matured and may no longer fit in very well, or in quite the same way.

I remember another colleague, a teacher originally from

northern China, telling me long ago as 1971, during the days of the Great Proletarian Cultural Revolution, that retiring in China proper was a real possibility for him. He has, in fact, retired in the United States. In my own case, in the first instance, I intended going back to England. Then my wife and I planned on Australia. In the end, we have remained in Hong Kong.

In our survey, something like seventeen per cent of the 81 couples questioned had already retired in Hong Kong, although some travel frequently and live elsewhere for sizeable periods every year. Other couples not yet retired intimated they would quite likely retire in Asia, probably in Hong Kong.

Several couples were considering choosing between Hong Kong and Mainland China. One young husband said about his Chinese wife:

> *It's always been her dream to live in Mainland China. She hopes we can retire there. Personally, I would prefer a lovely, old historic city like Edinburgh.*

Another more mature couple, consisting of an American who is fluent in Putonghua and his northern Chinese wife, wrote:

> *We would like to retire somewhere in China, such as in Shekou situated just to the north-west of Hong Kong, or Shanghai. Hong Kong is too expensive.*

But a Briton felt that living in China and following a purely Chinese Mainland lifestyle, what with its language limitations, may not be suitable for many Europeans.

One couple with retirement looming only a couple of years away, phrased it this way:

> *We expect to live in Hong Kong on retirement*
> *primarily because, warts and all, we are happy*
> *here. I think Hong Kong is one of the most exciting*
> *places on earth to live and work. You always get the*
> *impression you're at the cutting edge. There's always*
> *plenty going on.*

About one-fifth of the respondents in our survey consisted of relatively young couples, many of whom had no idea yet where they would retire. As one respondent wrote, 'God only knows!'

A number of young couples said they hoped to be able to divide their time, in varying proportions, between one or two places, such as England, Switzerland, France, Canada, Ireland, Continental Europe, Hong Kong or Singapore. One couple said they would continue to live in Hong Kong, but that they would spend a couple of months a year in their second home, in Sweden, feeling it necessary to go back to Europe for their 'cultural fix' every so often. There were others who said they hoped, or had already decided to retire in Canada, New Zealand, Australia or the United States. This young couple seemed to be thinking aloud:

> *We expect to go back to the United Kingdom where*
> *we have a couple of properties, and friends who*
> *sing and play guitar, which we did previously.*

But taxation is high there and it is cold. We could consider Mainland China, where the cost of living is lower, but there seems to be more crime there, and who knows how stable it will be? The decision is largely practical in nature, with an eye to the children's prospects.

chapter seven
discrimination

If you don't behave and be good, that *gwaipoh* over there will take you away!

An American woman in Hong Kong

When asked about whether they as a couple had experienced any discrimination, fifty-eight per cent of the respondents said a straightforward 'No' or possibly added a few words to cover themselves, 'Not knowingly', 'Not really', 'No, not at all. Maybe we have been lucky', or 'No, I am not aware of this happening, but I'm sure some people held discriminatory views.' 'Not in Boston,' said one respondent, 'people are pretty liberal and open-minded here.' A British solicitor in Hong Kong said, 'No,' but went on to say except for 'official barriers' to Chinese wives being issued with British passports.

If this survey was conducted in the 1950s or 60s, the responses would have been significantly different. In the southern United States, the colour bar kept blacks and whites apart, and in Hong Kong, there were days when the Hong Kong and Shanghai Bank, now renamed HSBC, did not normally employ Chinese other than as janitors and minor staff. Clerks, typists and secretaries were usually Eurasians or local Portuguese, with a few Europeans. Sir Jimmy McGregor, a retired Hong Kong civil servant now living in Vancouver, told *M Magazine* about his courtship and marriage during this time:

> [I met my wife] *in 1955, but in those days it was quite rare for Chinese to marry gwailos. We didn't marry until 1963 because her family, her mother especially, was horrified at the prospect of her daughter marrying a foreigner. When I was dating her, people used to stare at us. It was really not the done thing back then.*

In another case a Briton, also a government servant, started dating a Chinese woman in late 1955. As the news got around, there was resistance among his European colleagues and his boss tried to have him dismissed from the government service, but was told by the Colonial Secretariat officers, in late 1956, that, as the officer's work was of a good standard, this was not possible. A certain amount of ostracism by Western colleagues took place, but interestingly not by most Chinese colleagues who felt the Europeans were being unreasonable. The Chinese say, 'Sweep away the snow in front of your own door, do not bother about the snow on your neighbours' roof' (各家自掃門前雪，不管他人瓦上霜). Even though this is a northern saying, Cantonese know it as well. In other words, 'mind your own business!' Yet the European boss said to the officer:

> *'I realise if you were getting a divorce and marrying another European, no one would object. But, the*

fact that you are going to marry a Chinese cannot be accepted. All right, you can say this is not fair. But there it is.'

Eventually, they were married in 1960. All Chinese colleagues who were invited attended the wedding, but some European colleagues declined. At Christmas, 1961, the officer received a card from his boss, 'Peace on earth, good will to all men.' Although from then on the boss accepted the marriage, a certain amount of bad feeling continued in the workplace, especially from a few of the British wives.

A Chinese woman with a Scottish husband confirmed that things were certainly worse in early post-World War Two Hong Kong:

These days [at the start of the third millennium] *there is no discrimination at all. In the early 1970s, there was still prejudice in Hong Kong against Chinese women being seen with non-Chinese men with discriminatory and insulting remarks sometimes being made by Chinese observers.*

One English husband in Hong Kong also wrote that he felt there had been a change of attitude since the early 1960s, when he married, and a fellow Briton there said he had also been looked down upon occasionally in the past, but less so these days. 'Or maybe I'm less sensitive now that I'm older. Today, far fewer people are concerned about Western-Chinese marriages. A New Zealand man, nevertheless went so far as to say that being non-Chinese in Hong Kong is always an issue:

'We as a mixed couple are looked at, but we do not care. The same thing happens in New Zealand. There is more anti-Asian thinking there.'

One old Shanghainese, now dead, a long time European resident of old Shanghai, used to say he was delighted in walking past a group of Europeans with a beautiful Chinese woman on his arm, just to upset them! Meanwhile, a Shanghainese wife recalled the stares she used to receive especially in the late 1960s and 70s when she was with her British boyfriend, and then husband; she thought that people saw them as being on a 'one-night stand.' Certainly, stares and double stares were often the name of the game in those days. It is interesting to note that this woman had previously said that she had never knowingly been slighted!

Discrimination can be even more pronounced when the man is Chinese and the woman Western, although Chinese men seemed to be more reticent about reporting any discrimination in the survey. Elsie Tu, previously Mrs Elliott, writes in her recent book, *Shouting at the Mountain*, about when she was walking in Hong Kong, with Andrew Tu, who later became her husband (Tu, 2004:191). When she was delayed in the crowd, or stopped to look in a shop window, Andrew would continue walking and she sometimes would lose sight of him. She was puzzled about his behaviour. We are talking about the 1960s Hong Kong when, as Elsie phrases it, 'his world understood mine as little as my world understood his.' In those days, it was hardly conceivable that there was a legitimate reason for a Chinese man to walk beside a European woman. They must be 'up to no good'. Thus, when Andrew was walking together with Elsie, he often felt terribly embarrassed, with people staring and wondering!

This poem, set in a very Chinese neighbourhood of Hong Kong in 1988, communicates a similar experience:

Looking

When he puts his loved
brown hand on her
loved white arm

men on noodle shop stools
stare
why-don't-you-have-a-Chinese-girlfriend
monologues

women who know their beauty
give body-looks at him
her
then her again
and make a sum of it

entire eyes come
from tiger balm pajamas
men and women in metal
history elevators which have never
carried a Chinese man with a White woman
(Slavick, 2004:58)

Another English husband recalls an unpleasant experience with his Chinese wife as they checked into the Great Eastern Hotel, a business hotel next to the Liverpool Street Railway Station in London, in August 1963. The receptionist, an English woman, did her best to avoid giving the couple a room, and then slammed their passports down on the counter. Strangely enough, after checking in, the other hotel staff were all pleasant. It seemed to bear out some people's belief that men can be less domineering and race conscious than women, although generalisations can be dangerous. In the survey, there were several couples who felt discomfort from or discrimination by British women, in particular.

Inter-racial couples travelling in Mainland China have experienced difficulty with accommodation, especially on a tight budget. Over the years, some smaller hotels simply have not been open to foreigners, and no amount of coaxing could change that fact. A marriage certificate has even been required.

But it takes all sorts and one couple in our survey, this time a Western man and a Chinese woman, wrote that they were not aware of any discriminatory slights. In fact, just the opposite:

> *Many people are curious and interested in our very obvious differences, particularly people in Hong Kong and China, but also people in the United Kingdom.*

'No, I have not been looked down upon personally because of my mixed marriage,' said a Malaysian Chinese woman living in England. She went on to say that racism happens everywhere, and she was not bothered about people's opinions in the slightest. Like many people, she believes that the best way to fend it off is by putting on a bold front. Some, especially British born Chinese, often known as 'BBCs', for example, believe, 'You have got to stick up for yourself.' Others, who desperately want to 'fit in' in overseas communities, may play down racism (Parker, 1995:107).

Imagined racial slights obviously occur, as do imagined class discrimination slights. It seems apparent that while some spouses are aware of racist remarks, either real or implied, their partners, for whatever reason, remain oblivious. It has been repeated many times that, when one Englishman opens his mouth another Englishman hates him, depending on whether he or she speaks the Queen's English, or with a Scottish, north country, cockney or whatever accent, although such discrimination applies less today. In a similar way, some Hong Kong Chinese tend to consider that they are superior to Mainland Chinese.

A Shanghainese girl of fifteen was given advice by her uncle in the 1960s: 'Do not marry a Cantonese, do not marry a foreigner, and, most important of all, do not marry a Jew' (Wei, 1981). Meanwhile, a Cantonese woman said her father never really got over the shock when she married a Shanghainese. He would not have had any difficulty if she had married a European, as he had worked as a civil servant in Hong Kong for many years with Britons, for whom he had respect. Even within one province, there can be a hierarchy of sorts: residents of some counties of Guangdong take on varying status levels, at least in some people's minds, and Hong Kong Chinese residents tend to look down upon people, Chinese or otherwise, with darker skin. Many Chinese women go out of their way to protect themselves from the sun by using parasols and wearing hats.

Historically, the Chinese have been convinced throughout their long, continuous civilisation that their country was the centre of the universe. Consider its name for itself: 'central country' (中央國家), or the more typical translation, 'Middle Kingdom'. The Chinese called 'other' people, Mongolians to Britons, 'barbarians' (野蠻人) and considered them inherently inferior. Unfortunately, old tribal loyalties and patriotism can frequently develop into chauvinism and racism. The British and Americans have been frequently accused of this as well throughout the years of the Empire, and the 'War on Terror' today, for instance.

Harry Lee has long objected to being called by his English forename and prefers to be known as Lee Kuan Yew. His ideas about race include that the elderly like to see their grandchildren grow up in their own likeness, and that the continuity of the flesh and spirit should be an unending chain. When a Chinese marries a Westerner, this chain is broken. In a speech to parliament, on 23 February 1977, the senior statesman of Singapore, Lee Kuan Yew, professed that he understood the Englishman (Minchin, 1986:254-5).

> *'He knows deep in his heart he is superior to the Welshman and the Scotsman. Deep here* [sic]*, I am a Chinaman. Yes, an uprooted Chinaman*

transformed into a Singaporean.'

One would think that Chinese who have lived a long time in the West would be more ready to accept their children marrying Caucasians. Although figures are hard to come by, one study in 1990 revealed that as many as twenty-seven per cent of Chinese in New York City, for instance, had married outside their own race (Sung,1990:10). But acceptance is by no means the norm. I am reminded of a third-generation American-Chinese man who insists that, although ethnic Chinese, he is a patriotic American who has served in the United States Army. Wedged between two cultures, he is undoubtedly still immensely proud of being Chinese, and if he suspects any racial slur, is prepared to throw a punch. In his own marriage, he had no intention of 'mixing the breed' and with the help of matchmakers, visited Hong Kong in the early 1960s to find a 'real Chinese wife'. The wedding took place in the Crown Colony and a month later, the bride followed her husband to the States where he re-established himself as a Chinese. His wife, expected to sinicise the family, bore him four sons and a daughter who were brought up speaking Chinese, and were very aware of their roots.

Later, he threw his adult daughter out of the house. 'With one stroke of the knife' (一刀兩斷) and forbade the sons from speaking to her, all because she had a Caucasian boyfriend. He made it very clear that he did not want Eurasian grandchildren, and could not bear the thought of her, his only daughter, sleeping with a 'foreign devil', even within the confines of marriage. Later, she married a different Western man, and her father eventually relented, and is at least outwardly at peace with the couple. Now in retirement, he lives in an up-market section of a city in the United States and spends much of his time in Chinatown.

Views about cross-cultural marriage held by Hong Kong Chinese vary considerably. One Chinese woman anthropologist, in her late twenties, holds the view that, although many Chinese parents may not openly oppose their children marrying Westerners, at heart most do not welcome the idea. This was confirmed by a group of three Chinese marriage counsellors, in their forties, whom I interviewed. All of them said their parents would have objected if they themselves had told them they were going to marry a Westerner. The opposition more often than not comes from the fathers. Mothers, on the whole, are more sympathetic and understanding, as are well-educated parents. If the daughter is well educated and speaks good English, both parents seem to be more likely to respect her views and accept her 'marrying out'.

I questioned a number of Hong Kong Chinese in their teens and twenties about how their parents would react to them having a Western spouse. In most cases, the youngsters told me their parents would not like it. One woman did say she had dated three Western men and that her parents, who had only primary school education, did not object; in fact, they believed that if the Caucasian husband had a good steady job, she would have enhanced her status. She added that her parents opposed her sister marrying a Japanese man, though as recollections of World War Two atrocities against the Chinese and others are still vivid. Chinese are also usually strongly opposed to their children marrying Indians or blacks, largely because of their dark skin. Such views are decidedly racist. As a whole, the author does feel that more Chinese people, particularly parents and grandparents are against inter-racial marriage than for, but there are no figures to back this up.

With, for instance, some Chinese fathers being unable to come to terms with the idea of their daughters marrying Westerners, the physical, sexual side of marriage seems to be important. Although they may not be outright racist as such, many do not like the idea of 'mixing the breed', and many cannot bear the thought of a big, hairy, sweaty Westerner sleeping with their beloved daughter. Some Chinese boyfriends do not like the idea of their Chinese partners having previously dated Westerners. One Chinese woman university graduate, who had studied in the United States, said that when she returned to Hong Kong, her Chinese boyfriend tried to find out if she had had Western boyfriends there. To some extent, the 'macho thing' is in operation: not only can men of one race be seen as having 'control' over women of another race, but also a dominance over the men by being able to take their women away from them.

To continue with the physical aspects, there is a widespread belief that European's penis is bigger than the Chinese, and in the West, it is often said that the average black man has the largest. One Chinese woman in the survey was told by her mother shortly before the wedding that she need not worry because the vagina was capable of expanding to accommodate all sizes. The size of the penis is considered to be important in many societies, including in the Chinese society. An imagined epidemic, known as *koro* broke out more than once during the latter half of the twentieth century in Singapore: the penis is said to shrink and retract into the abdomen. In Hong Kong, there are many email advertisements these days about enlarging the penis, with such headings as, 'Be the guy the girls tell their friends about!'

In the Hong Kong newspaper, the *South China Morning Post*, on 23 April 2005, it was reported that the Director of the Union Hospital's Urology Centre, Chan Leung-wai, said, 'Basically our conclusion is that Hong Kong men's penises are not worse [sic] than our Western counterparts.' The Director's team 'sized up' 148 ethnic Chinese volunteers, and dispelled an enduring myth forever.

A Western woman in Paris, when she mentioned in passing that her husband was from Mainland China, received a strange reaction:

> *I was chatting with a Parisian man and in the course of the conversation, it came out that my husband was Chinese. He didn't look impressed. A strange look crossed his face, and he asked me in not very tactful French: What's it like making love to a Chinese? I deigned* [not] *to reply.*

In 'The Best Lovers East or West?' a centre-page spread article in the *Sunday Morning Post*, on 20 March 1994, the following views were expressed by four women in Hong Kong, the first three married to a Chinese man, the last to a Westerner:

European wife Crystal Li: The Chinese have a long and rich sexual tradition. They have learned massage and acupuncture. They know all the right points of pleasure on a woman's body.

European Sally Lo: Chinese men are reserved and they have a highly developed sensitivity towards other people's feelings.

English widow Elsie Tu: Chinese men look better than Westerners. They carry age well. They have lovely small bones, and their hair is strong and beautifully dark. Oh, their eyes are very attractive.

Chinese Lan Ying 'Sunshine' Coats remarked 'Chinese girls who marry Chinese men seem to live much more limited, traditional lives. They are busy making babies and worrying about money.' She went on to say she was born into a traditional Hong Kong Chinese family, and never dreamed she would marry a *gwailo*. She said the future of her sex life was straightforward: she would remain a virgin until she married, then she would have children. 'The role of a Chinese wife is not to have wonderful sex, but to have wonderful babies. He was so different compared to my Chinese boyfriends. His views about sex were different, too. To him, it was more about sharing and enjoying each other. To me, it was something a man did to a woman, not something to enjoy together. I had to keep quiet about our sex life before we married. My Chinese girl friends never talked about sex.'

Sunshine's view is, of course, the traditional, old

fashioned view, and is perhaps not too unlike the attitudes of a married Chinese woman, in the mid 1930s, who pulled her nightdress up over her head so she could not see what was going on. One English husband wrote in his survey that among the wedding presents given by his Chinese in-laws and his *amah*, when he married in Hong Kong in the 1960s, was a white handkerchief for wiping private parts when the bride's hymen was broken. The handkerchief was sometimes kept as a family 'heirloom'. Stress is still placed on virginity and, by tradition, if a bride was found not to be a virgin, she was sent back to her natal family. At a wedding banquet, her virginity is signified by the serving of crisp, golden-brown, suckling pig. Sleeping with a virgin is supposed to be beneficial. The man can absorb her *chi* (氣) [life-force]. According to a Taoist belief, male and female energy forces complement each other.

Continuing with experiences of couples living in Hong Kong, a Chinese woman in our survey said:

> [I am] *a Chinese married to a European. Once a Chinese colleague sitting right next to me openly stated that it was bad to marry gweilos.*

A British male teacher added:

> *British female school teachers in Hong Kong often look down on any man who marries an Asian girl. But apart from that, I have experienced no discrimination.*

This remark may correspond with the hotel incident in London, in 1963, where a British woman had been so openly

unhelpful towards a Western-Chinese couple, as well with
the experience of a Chinese civil engineer who is married to a
German woman. They are adamant that many English wives in
Hong Kong avoided talking with them.

An American woman married to a Chinese, who divides
her time between the United States and Asia, wrote:

> In my opinion, and as far as I know, I have never
> in America or anywhere else been discriminated
> against or looked down upon because of my mixed
> marriage. However, I do feel I have been looked
> down upon in Hong Kong and discriminated
> against for being a Westerner. It has not happened
> recently but in the past, since I understand
> Cantonese very well, I could hear mothers on
> buses or on trains scolding their misbehaving
> children and saying:. If you don't behave and be
> good, that gwaipoh [ghost woman] over there
> will take you away! I heard this several times
> each time in slightly different circumstances. I
> feel that children are being taught sometimes to
> fear Westerners. Anyway, years ago I felt there
> was more discrimination towards Westerners.
> Nowadays, I rarely feel or notice any at all.

A Chinese woman in the survey relayed:

> Some Hong Kong Chinese have asked me what it
> is like to be married to an Englishman, and there
> might have been an element of incredulity in their
> questions, as though it was highly peculiar of me to

*make this choice. Since it is always people of little
education or sophistication who ask such question,
I have ascribed their inquisitiveness and possible
discrimination to their profound ignorance of any
other cultures and therefore take no account of it.*

Is excessive curiosity a kind of discrimination? One
Chinese woman with a Welsh husband wrote that 'people show
curiosity more than prejudice because the two of us are so
different, both in types and looks', while an Australian woman
who lived with her Chinese husband's family in Hong Kong
writes of curiosity mixing with discrimination:

*As you will understand, in the 1970s there were
not a lot of mixed marriages as they were called
then. My marriage was within a very traditional
Chinese family who I felt were very good to me.
I was just different! I don't think I was totally
discriminated against. Chinese girls in the
1970s were related to the 'Suzy Wong world'.
My husband and I are probably looked upon
in today's society, similarly, as we have a special
needs child and that causes additional stares of,
maybe concern, and even more confusion. I feel
this is discrimination for the three of us. As I'm
older now, I don't let it affect our family, but I
accept it as just one of the difficulties of living in
Hong Kong.*

Few respondents discussed experiences in Mainland
China. One Chinese wife wrote that she was upset about this
instance of racial prejudice:

Yes [we were discriminated against]*, particularly looked down upon by some of my own fellow Chinese who thought I married my husband for his passport. In Canada, any discrimination I experienced had nothing to do with my marriage.*

In another case, a mature student married one of her teachers in the run up to the change of sovereignty of Hong Kong in 1997. They settled in England. When they had rows, the Chinese woman used to scold him and say, 'I only married you so I could get a British passport!' Meanwhile, the Chinese husband of a European wife, in South Africa in about 1990, was told by a Taiwanese couple that European women only marry for money.

One couple intimated they had not really been discriminated against, but the European husband likes to joke and say that, regardless of realities, when they are out together they have typical stereotype looks of the rich gwailo husband and the pretty, brainless Chinese woman pasted all over them, an attitude, they say, which is particularly noticeable in Mainland China. Another European recalls overhearing an elderly Chinese male politely saying, several years ago, that Westerners attract all the prettiest Chinese girls!

On the assumption that all Westerners are wealthy, one Chinese woman says she always tells her husband, although an Old Hong Kong Hand, not to go shopping on his own for he will be charged higher *gwailo* prices.

One Western woman recounted her worst experience,

which happened in 1992, at Zhongshan University, a very reputable institution in the city of Guangzhou. A group of Chinese women students had been in the habit of getting together with her one night a week, for a nice long talk. After she married, they abruptly stopped coming:

> *It was not because there was a man in the house.*
> *We lived in two separate cities for eight months*
> *after our marriage. Also, I was alone on weekday*
> *evenings. It was just that these young Chinese*
> *ladies on the Mainland did not seem to be able to*
> *handle our mixed marriage situation.*

Most of the time, however, she said that when people had any initial reservation about her marriage, it dissolved once they met her Mainland Chinese husband, and they would be welcomed. Other couples were upset at times by remarks made by persons on whom they thought they could rely. For instance, a Welshman wrote:

> *Nothing serious* [concerning racism], *although I*
> *was annoyed some years ago when a colleague, and*
> *a person I had considered an intelligent friend,*
> *spoke of the problems of 'miscegenation'.*

A Chinese woman said:

> *Yes, I have sensed such an attitude from some people,*
> *but I always tell myself that I would not want to be*
> *friends with anyone so narrow-minded. Over the*
> *years I have been in social situations when people*
> *have criticised the Chinese quite rudely and then*
> *half-heartedly apologised when they remember that*

my husband is Chinese.

A European woman takes up the point:

Yes, we both think we have been discriminated against. Even some of our own friends do not like mixed marriages.

When interviews were conducted with Chinese and Eurasians in 1990s London by David Parker, a Eurasian doctoral student, one woman explained why she would not marry a British man: she said she was afraid how her children would turn out. Another woman said she was afraid her parents would disown her if her children were not full-blooded Chinese. Parker said that, during discussions, this topic led to an awkward situation with people distinctly uncomfortable about expressing their views. Some felt inhibited. He wrote there was some shifting of positions and a search for common ground. And, at one stage, he was told that he had been spoken to by the Chinese as if he was English. His reply was, 'But what about when you told me you hated the English?' They answered, 'Well, I suppose we thought you were on our side.'

Later on, Parker and the group of interviewees went to a Chinese restaurant where there were a number of Eurasian children. On seeing them, the pure Chinese members in Parker's group pointed at them saying, 'Isn't that terrible?'

Certainly mixed-blood children often attract attention, either positive or negative. This view was expressed time and again in the survey: Eurasian children are frequently good looking, talented, and their bilingual skills serve them well. As one European respondent said, 'Not just with my children. I have noticed it with other mixed marriages. The children seem to be very attractive and well balanced. Is it in the genes? There are those who firmly believe Eurasian children are, on average, more intelligent and more creative than single-race youngsters, and because of their dual heritage and global lifestyle they may not just be bicultural, but multicultural. They can move without difficulty from one mindset to another' (Romano, 2001:125).

The physical appearance of Eurasians can vary considerably. A small percentage looks either almost totally Chinese or almost totally European, while the majority fit somewhere along the continuum between the two extremes.

One loving couple in their questionnaire wrote:

Wife: *I like our baby, who is mixed of course, because he is cute.*

Husband: *It seems strange that the shape of our baby's eyes is different to mine.*

Approximately one-third of the respondents in our survey also said their children had no difficulty settling in at school and getting along with classmates. One or two reported that their children initially had trouble, but that it could happen with children of any nationality, anywhere.

One British father reported that his Eurasian daughter had difficulty settling into a school in Australia, but commented:

'A few unfortunate incidents seemed mainly to be evidence of the social and economic problems there.'

Looking at another case, this time in Hong Kong, between an American father and a northern, Mainland Chinese mother:

I do not think my wife nor I have ever been discriminated against, but then we seldom placed ourselves in such situations where such discrimination could manifest itself. However, despite or perhaps because of the enriched gene pool, I do think our mixed-race children were discriminated against in school, particularly our son. He was rather bright academically but not well accepted by some European teachers or European classmates. In reaction, he went out of his way to cultivate an acceptable British accent and not to speak too much Chinese nor speak to Chinese classmates.

Later, when the school put his name forward for scholarship recognition awards in citywide competitions, we found the judges felt perhaps he was not Chinese enough. I do not want to make more of this than it was. All things considered, Hong Kong has not been a bad place at all to raise children. At least children from mixed marriages here have the potential to grow up speaking two or three different languages. This would not be true in the United States. The gift of multi-lingualism is probably one of the greatest gifts that parents can pass on to their children. It can be done in Hong Kong with relative ease.

Meanwhile, a male Anglo-Scot offered:

In particular, our children have been extremely well received at school in Hong Kong and I have not been able to detect any racism. This is surprising to me. I feel that there would probably have been some racism in a school in Britain.

Before a Shanghainese woman sent her two sons off to a boarding school in England, she taught them to say, 'Yes, I'm Eurasian. My mother is Chinese. I have the best of both worlds.'

In spite of some racism in Britain, many children seem to adjust quite well as this lovely little poem (Alibhai-Brown, 2001:97), composed by nine-year old primary school pupil George Richelieu, illustrates:

I'm not black and I'm not white
I'm my own colour and that's all right.
A colour is something I cannot change
A colour is something with a very big range.
But I'm not black and I'm not white
I'm my own colour, and that's all right.

While on the subject of colour, with a number of mixed race children in Britain being described as 'beige' in colour, an Englishman in our survey wrote about what he described as the concept of 'racial distance' between people. In Britain, it is not unusual to have dark and fair people in the same family. But it does not seem to constitute a problem. The husband went on:

*Since I have dark hair and eyes, the 'racial distance'
between my Chinese wife and me does not make
us stand out in a crowd. However a blonde man
who married a black woman would be much more
manifestly mixed and this would probably trigger
occasional racial comments which might be hurtful.
Whatever our own attitudes, we cannot change the
stereotypes present in the world at large.*

When it comes to racism in the West, the fairer-skinned
Chinese have always had an advantage, compared to the darker-
skinned races. A Chinese woman who has lived in England
since the early 1950s and raised Eurasian children there, said:

*Of course there is some racism in Britain. There is
racism to some degree everywhere. But racism is not
so bad towards the Chinese in the United Kingdom
as it is for some other nationalities, towards blacks
and Pakistanis, for example.*

Yasmin Alibhai-Brown in her book, *Mixed Feelings: The
Complex Lives of Mixed Race Britons*, gives a number of examples
of the abuse that blacks and Pakistanis occasionally experience.
A white mother recounted on the radio programme, *Woman's
Hour*, how an Englishman reacted towards her:

'He looked at my fourteen-month-old child in
the pushchair and said, 'Another f *****g nigger,
another f *****g coon'.'

In fact, the mother of an Englishman, who has always
been very kind and helpful to his Chinese wife, had once asked

him before the marriage, 'Why don't you marry a nice English girl?' Although said in a pleasant way, her son has always felt she meant what she said.

Another Western husband said that in marriage, the commonality of ideals, backgrounds and goals significantly outscore issues of race. A lot of the time, the pressures and differences a couple feels are not actually generated from the marriage partners, but from the narrow-mindedness of other people. One couple in Hong Kong, who apparently had problems in this regard, said:

> *It is crazy to be stared at during a meal in a restaurant because we as a couple are not of the same race. We think those who should be filling in this questionnaire, on dealing with differences of race, should be certain members of the general public rather than us!*

adventure?

The 'wrestling' and 'handling' of conflicts have provided a rich and powerful force that bind, in our case, an out-of-the-ordinary type marriage.

A Hong Kong Chinese woman

At its best, a cross-cultural marriage is the 'best of both worlds', with the couple enjoying a richness of cultural diversity. Learning a new language, becoming familiar with a new culture and customs, meeting people one never would have had the opportunity to know before – an endless potential for a colourful and fascinating married life, if one is receptive, meets the challenges, crosses the hurdles, takes advantage of the opportunities, and in essence, lives the adventure! Many couples in the survey would not have it any other way. Our marriage has been an 'exciting voyage of discovery' said one respondent.

When questioned whether a cross-cultural marriage has as much chance of success and happiness as a same-culture marriage, the respondents generally felt the likelihood was the same. It is personalities that clash, not necessarily cultures, and one husband admitted, 'My wife and I are both "difficult" people anyway!' Another man clarified that, 'Any rows we have had are normal marital problems. Cultural differences have never been a hurdle at all.' Other spouses added, 'It depends on what kind of person one is rather than blaming one's culture, and, just a question really, could cultural factors actually be an excuse for common or garden marriage problems?' Marriage is based on love, understanding and respect for one's partner. 'Cross culture adds another dimension [resulting in] advantages and disadvantages. It is more a matter of "dealing with" and "learning from" difficulties.' A husband living in London was reminded of Theodore Roosevelt's motto: 'The single most important ingredient of success is an ability to get on with people.'

The general consensus was that spouses need to be mindful that they each come from a different culture, and then adapt accordingly, make allowances, and extend effort. To paraphrase an Anglo-Scottish man who wrote in some detail, every marriage faces hurdles and every healthy marriage surely has a way to clear those hurdles; the extra ones presented by cultural differences may weaken the marital bond, or may trigger the necessary adjustments to make the bond stronger.

The majority said that additional hurdles may exist in cross-cultural marriages, yes, but it is 'a different type of "hurdle", not necessarily an extra one', and then normally only 'initially... until your spouse's culture is better understood'. 'Yes and no,' another spouse qualified. 'It means more work on communicating, but marriage is all about communicating and "putting up with each other" anyway.' To one spouse, the word 'challenge' is preferred to 'hurdle', more effort is needed, more understanding, and a healthy amount of 'respect for each other' [and the other's culture] is a key consideration. With time and effort, the couples felt, most problems can be resolved: the stress on the need to extend effort came over in varying forms, repeatedly. The proverb of Roy L. Smith seems to apply: 'The ideal marriage is not one in which two people marry to be happy. But to make each *other* happy' (Gomes, 2003, front cover).

People who answered this interview question at greater length – about 80 per cent of the respondents – offered such thoughtful responses as this Australian wife:

> *All marriages have hurdles all the time. Different cultures probably add to the difficulties and mean working harder to understand 'why'. There seem to be so many things to understand, and how we accept them and deal with them and make the marriage harmonious or discordant. My husband and I have faced many 'hurdles' and probably will face many more.*

A Swedish man felt that real 'hurdles' occur when the husband and the wife are unable to communicate in a common language, and when they originate from two completely different lifestyles, have different standards of education, and are too stubborn to be able to compromise. One Chinese woman wrote in a similar vein, 'A harmonious marriage has more to do with compatible lifestyles and similar interests. My husband considers different cultures as a very low hurdle, certainly not a high one.'

One spouse was curious about the statistics, saying

'my impression is that both kinds of marriages [cross-cultural and same culture marriages] fail with more or less equal frequency. If cross-cultural marriages are more likely to fail, an Anglo-Scottish man conjectured, this may be because they are statistically more likely to be marriages of convenience.[15]

The Anglo-Scot continued with this scenario: if a woman marries a wealthier and older man from a more successful environment, the arrangement may be fine while the motivation lasts, but motivation easily changes in a relationship. If personal values are different, which is likely, then the couple may find that their children will bind them closer: it may actually accentuate the gap. On the other hand, if two people marry largely because they find each other's value system to be agreeable, then that may provide them with a strong cement against destabilising forces and a good base for bringing up children of whom they may be proud.

The husband said that he and his Chinese wife believe that true happiness is very much related to 'personal culture', 'We have seen couples who do not get on because one or both adhere to their national cultures and they are not prepared to adjust in a flexible way.' 'This might be a problem,' he continued, 'if someone needs to be part of an organised cultural system in order to feel 'comfortable'. He went on:

> However my wife and I are both people who make
> up our own minds on what is right and what is
> wrong. We have developed the habit of talking
> through moral issues and reaching agreement where
> justice lies.

This emphasis on an independent way of thinking comes through in advice offered by several couples in various ways: 'one should not care too much what other people think'. 'Marry the person you love,' one husband wrote, 'other people may draw conclusions about you or categorise you in some way because of your marriage partner, but that is their problem, not yours.' Or, remembering Thoreau, 'If a man does not keep pace with his companions, perhaps it is because he hears a different drummer. Let him march to the music he hears.'

This maturity, strength and openness make room for an intelligent understanding, as is echoed in the survey:

> *Much depends on the backgrounds of the two persons involved. If one comes from a well travelled and 'culturally open' family, the chances of success in a mixed marriage are greater than if one comes from a closed, provincial background.*

In fact, several couples have lived in each others' countries. One well-travelled couple said, 'Both of us are not native-culture concentrics but "comfortable" in both Chinese and Western cultures.' A British husband living in Australia went into some detail:

> *In the case of my wife and I, for reasons of high exposure to each other's culture, it is almost like a marriage of people from the same culture, with a lot of icing on the cake! I imagine that a cross-cultural marriage at the other end of the spectrum, with a vast amount of mutual ignorance of the other's language and culture, has a lot against it being a*

success. Generally, also learning about the other person's culture is a potential bonus but often it becomes just an extra variable to be wrestled with. And with marriages to a Chinese, there is so much variation across the vast country as a whole.

Spouses in any marriage, whether they are from different cultures or well-travelled or not, may not always share the same views on how to handle anger, grief, sadness, frustration, worry, loneliness, conflict and death. A partner may be puzzled by the way the spouse deals with the situation at hand. T. G. Evans, who lived a rural Chinese lifestyle in Hong Kong's New Territories, wrote to the Editor of the *Hong Kong Standard* under the heading, 'It takes time to know the Chinese.' 'There are times when my [Chinese wife and] family and I differ. In the past this was often. But after many years of marriage, it is now very rare.' (Evans, 1984) Yet one elderly respondent in the survey wrote, 'It does seem Chinese and Westerners think differently.'

To take a somewhat theoretical approach, it has been suggested that Asians tend to think in complex, contextual, holistic, and all-embracing ways, first considering the overall, perhaps wide-ranging, fields of interest and then narrowing this down, although options are, if possible, left open, until segments are analysed and items pinpointed (Waters, 1991:35). When a Chinese writes an address in the traditional way, the country comes first, working down to the street address and the addressee last. Similarly with dates, the year is written first and the day last. In Chinese landscape paintings, too, more attention is paid to the image as a whole rather than to the details, such as tiny figures. Chinese medicine also takes a holistic approach, whereas the traditional Western approach tends to concentrate more on the specific malfunctioning part of the anatomy.

Again, there is a difference in the concept of time. The Westerner tends to see it stretching out in a straight, linear path, while the non-westernised Chinese as a spiral (Waters, 1991:35). This may have something to do with the belief in reincarnation, and the acceptance that there is 'a time to live and a time to die, and a time to be born again'. This view of time has other implications. When an opportunity is missed, a Westerner might see it receding steadily into the past, while a Chinese person might, inwardly, expect that on occasions in the future, on the helical of time, there will again be similar opportunities within easy reach. With such a philosophy, stress can be reduced.

Westerners, it has been suggested, are largely left-lobe logical thinkers, who take a more systematic and rational approach: linear, sequential, systematic, and step by step. Contrastingly, Chinese are mainly right-hemisphere thinkers, with instinctive and simultaneous thought processes. They tend to see in wholes rather than in parts, to synthesise, not analyse.[16]

A Chinese wife was one of many spouses who added a good education to the list of qualities to help ensure that a cross-cultural marriage works:

> *Educated and worldly-experienced couples have a*
> *better chance of a happy cross-cultural marriage*

[16] One might ask what happens to a Chinese who is educated and raised in the West. Is it, in other words, nature or nurture? Again, what about the Eurasian? More research is needed on this fascinating topic.

being successful, as spouses are usually more tolerant and understanding towards each other.

It came across clearly in the questionnaires that some degree of parity of educational backgrounds and standards is beneficial for cross-cultural (and mono-cultural) marriages. There seems little doubt that this applies also for both class and social backgrounds. As an example (although both spouses were Chinese in this case), in the 1950s, an academic married the most famous night club singer in Hong Kong, against the advice of his headmaster father, who objected due to the fact that her educational standard was low and that the two had incompatible interests. After the couple settled into their new home, the husband often went out at night, preferring women who could provide intelligent company. Father's advice proved correct, the marriage was not a happy one.

An Englishman revealed:

I know many Englishmen, who are married to English women, are desperately unhappy. I also know men who have jumped into marriage with Filipina women, and ended up living in a flat with all her relatives. All things being equal, it is probably a little more difficult for cross-cultural marriages to survive. There are cultural differences and pressures which may not seem obvious at first, but are nevertheless there, and can cause misunderstandings and difficulties particularly at the beginning of a relationship. It helps if age and education gaps are not too wide.

This helps with any partnership.

Indeed, there were two marriages in the survey in which problems seemed to stem from differences in age, not culture. The first is an Englishman who confided about the difficulties he was facing:

> *Our marriage at present has a number of*
> *'hurdles'. It has become so because of diverse*
> *interests between my wife and I, and an age*
> *difference of sixteen years. Perhaps difficulties*
> *would have happened if even it had not been*
> *cross-cultural?*

The second is a divorcee from New Zealand:

> *I lay our marriage failure at the door of our big*
> *age difference, he* [my Chinese husband] *is*
> *younger than I, and the fact that we are not both*
> *Christians. Mind you, he refused to go and see a*
> *marriage guidance counsellor with me. That may*
> *have been something to do with 'saving face' in*
> *front of a stranger.* [17]

A Hong Kong Chinese woman, who has lived in the United States for many years with her American husband, said it took them several years to work out their cultural differences, but after that was done, there were no real problems. She believes it depends on the individuals concerned to make a relationship work, and it depends on how much time and energy the couple is prepared to invest. Another Hong Kong Chinese wife elaborates:

[17] *Many Westerners, men in particular, also resist counseling. An Australian woman told the author that many Australian men are reluctant to see a doctor, let alone a counsellor. She said a relative of hers refused to see a counsellor after the first session, because he felt 'humiliated'.*

*The 'wrestling' [with] and 'handling' of conflicts
have provided a rich and powerful force that
bind, in our case, an out-of-the-ordinary type
marriage. The closeness generated from a deep
understanding of each other makes it difficult
to entertain a third person in the relationship,
unless the third person is the wife's mother or the
couple's children. In the long term, the two of us
are self-sufficient within the relationship, revelling
in a sense of well-being when we are together.*

A happily married Englishman felt that 'women are more adaptable than men and can quickly come to terms with a new culture, particularly if their language skills are good and they are open-minded.' He went on to say that a good friend of his told him that once Chinese women marry, they somehow join the same 'trade union' as their husbands, and behave similarly whether the man is English, Chinese or Eskimo! He added:

*I have never thought of my wife as anything other
than a woman. Here ethnicity has never really
been significant in our marriage. All this has
gradually introduced new cultural elements to me
which have enriched my life, even though I am
still very English at heart.*

One Chinese woman echoes this idea in her remark, which she insisted in her survey, 'I have never considered I married a foreigner; I married John.' It seems that people in 'successful' marriages see the togetherness of two people and two cultures being an opportunity for richness and discovery, and for deeper understanding. One American spoke:

> *If you go into a mixed marriage sober, with your*
> *eyes open, you are probably a person who is going*
> *to be careful not to make too many cultural*
> *transgressions. You probably also are going to try*
> *to be culturally flexible. There is a presumption*
> *that you not only are marrying a spouse, but*
> *you are adopting a new culture about which you*
> *should be cautious and respectful.*

The other:

> *Intermarriage does not really add an extra*
> *hurdle. My husband and I have had a happy*
> *and harmonious marriage, and I do not feel that*
> *our different cultures have added any difficulties*
> *for us. For the most part, my husband and I*
> *have thrived on and enjoyed the differences*
> *between our two cultures.*

Many Chinese people are very proud of their heritage. I recall a middle-aged Chinese woman almost banging the table at a banquet, in a rather non-Chinese sort of way, as if she wanted to let us Westerners know how inferior we were, 'I'm so glad I'm Chinese,' she proclaimed, 'We have everything: history, art, culture, scenic beauty, you name it.'

There is much in what she said, of course. The Chinese anticipated the 'invention' of printing by Gutenberg and Caxton by about five centuries. They invented paper, including perfumed toilet paper for the imperial family in the fourteenth century, the compass, the making of steel and drilling for natural gas. They invented gunpowder, concocted mistakenly while looking for the elixir of life, and they developed intensive agriculture (Temple, 1986: passim).

Other firsts include the use of coal, mechanical clocks, suspension bridges, and lock gates. The Chinese invented deep drilling techniques, flame throwers, bells used in churches, fishing reels, an efficient horse harness which did not choke the poor animal, porcelain and map grids, paddle-wheel boats, watertight compartments, and rudders, just to name a few. The first toothbrush was made in China in the year 959 and 'reinvented' in Italy in the seventeenth century. Even the gondolas of Venice are, some believe, copies of China's Dragon Boats (龍舟), the design of which was said to have been taken to Europe by Marco Polo. With all of these achievements, and many more, why did the industrial revolution commence in Britain in the eighteenth century rather than in China in the thirteenth or fourteenth century when the 'Middle Kingdom' was well ahead of the West? Some believe it was, among other things, because there was abundant, cheap labour in China and the country's rapid technological progress by then had slowed. But all of this is another story (Waters, 1995:26 and 27: also Merson, 1990:passim).

Of course many English are proud of our country too, even if we do not have a national dress, unlike the Scots and many continental European countries. At Westminster, the English have the 'Mother of Parliaments'. At its peak, as every British schoolboy knew, the Empire, covered almost one-quarter of the globe. Although it is fashionable today to denigrate the

old Empire, the English transported our system of governance
to the far corners of the Earth. Today, at least seven hundred and
fifty million people speak English, although only barely half that
number speak it as their mother tongue (Graddol, 1996:12).
Indeed some estimates have put the figure at one billion.[18]

In recent years, the buzz word has been 'globalisation',
although some people prefer to call it 'Americanisation' which
in some instances has swept away all before it, with old cultures
and customs fallen into disuse. Forty years ago, McDonalds,
Kentucky Fried Chicken and Pizza Hut were not in Hong
Kong. Nor were there supermarkets. Instead, there was the tiny
compradore's or grocer's shop on the street corner. In more
recent years in our hi-tech world, Mainland China has copied
many such developments and crazes, so many of which started
in the United States.

United States is of course a vast country (though
not as vast as China) and a superpower, although China is
quickly establishing itself as such. Yet in spite of the amount
of Americanisation in Hong Kong over the past forty years,
the Chinese character remains, as does the legacy of the British
colonial administration for over a century and a half. One has
the opportunity to wander around districts like Sheung Wan,
where at Possession Point the British Union Jack was first
hoisted in 1841, and not far away is Man Mo Temple, which
was constructed about the same time as the Anglican Saint
John's Cathedral, at the end of the 1840s. There are also several
dilapidated but intriguing earth god shrines in this district of
Hong Kong Island.

[18] *Indeed it has frequently been quoted that more people speak Chinese every day than speak English. Nevertheless, in its present written form at least, with the difficulty of the characters and the tones, it is unlikely that Chinese will ever become a world language.*

Kowloon, on the Mainland of China, was ceded to Britain in 1860 in what was believed at the time to be perpetuity. Again there is much of interest there, including military history. The New Territories was leased to Britain for ninety-nine years, starting in 1898. This is the stamping ground of the Five Great Clans – and many smaller clans as well – with many well-preserved temples, ancestral and study halls, and much more. They have a long and proud history.[19]

It is not surprising then, that a city like Hong Kong with its tradition of East meeting West, is where so many Western-Chinese marriages and relationships have blossomed over the years. Also, because there is so much to learn in places like Hong Kong, and in China as a whole, it is not surprising that many couples in the survey admitted they had not taken full advantage of the unique opportunity. One Western husband said, 'When you put it like that, I've obviously been an under-achiever.' Another said guardedly, 'One never takes full advantage. But yes, I have taken advantage.' The same, of course, might apply to a Chinese spouse who wishes to learn about Western history and culture. One Chinese woman said, 'Yes, I have utilised some opportunities, but perhaps not as fully as I could have.'

She continued, 'My husband does not read or write Chinese but he does speak Cantonese.' Another woman sighed, 'My English husband has not persevered with improving his Cantonese, considering the time he has lived in a Chinese community.' A Swiss woman said that she could have made more effort to speak Cantonese more fluently, stressing that she regrets having given up an intensive university Mandarin course after two years. An English woman wrote:

> *I have worked extremely hard to learn the language and I find it very useful. I also find that most people I meet appreciate my efforts, and this enables me to integrate further.*

Most Westerners in the survey said that they had taken advantage of opportunities, even though many readily admitted that their knowledge of Chinese, Mandarin or Cantonese is limited. One man made a full confession: 'I am still completely unable to speak any Chinese. That is a real pity.' The overwhelming majority of Westerners in our survey, in fact, speak little or no Chinese, perhaps only ten per cent can read Chinese, and then only maybe two per cent at a high level.

Many Europeans living in places like Taiwan, Singapore and Hong Kong have a splendid opportunity to learn the Chinese language and about Chinese culture, but the difficulty for many people is that they move largely in Western circles, or among English-speaking Chinese. They live what they consider to be a reasonably full life without having to master Chinese. One Englishman is planning to address this issue:

> *I have clearly fallen short in not learning Cantonese properly, and this has had a serious effect on our family relationships and friendships. I am presently considering asking the family to switch to Cantonese at home, and also visiting China more often alone so that I am forced to speak Cantonese. This issue is important, and I*

would testify that couples should make a priority
of learning each others' languages, however much
effort it takes.

Many respondents, however, seemed to have accepted the fact that they would never learn the language. 'Too set in our cultural ways,' one replied. Some, including this Englishman, did not socialise with Chinese people much, yet alone learn the language:

It is easy to mix with Chinese people, although
I have never really succeeded anyway. But there
again, I have always worked with Westerners.

And a New Zealander:

I do not necessarily wish to simply do this or that
[only] because I have a Chinese wife. I prefer a
Western sense of humour and the companionship of
Westerners.

Such decisions are one's right, but a spouse must also appreciate the heritage and way of life of his or her spouse, at a basic level, at least. To do otherwise and to display an underlying contempt, is disrespectful and can certainly divide a marriage. This husband expresses a view that no one else in the survey put forward:

Confidence in the knowledge of one's own
culture is almost as important as toleration
and acceptance of one's spouse's culture in a
symmetrical 'I—thou' sort of way.

Another couple might have had some similar ideas in

their minds, when they wrote, 'We do support each other's cultural events and activities, but we keep our own separate cultural identities.'

Meanwhile, two men, an Englishman and a Welshman, admitted that in their cases, their Chinese wives had completely 'melded' into their culture. The Briton said, 'Advantage has been taken [of cultural opportunities] but there has never been time to take full advantage,' while the Welsh husband said that, on the whole his 'reasonable' number of pursuits into Chinese culture have been happy ones. An elderly Scottish man wrote about other ways of bridging the cultural divide:

> *Participating in local activities, such as mahjong,*
> *have given me much enjoyment which I otherwise*
> *would not have had.*

Again, the point was made that a European did not need to depend solely on his or her Chinese spouse to learn about the culture. A person who is keen to learn reads, engages in self study, joins clubs, attends lectures, visits historical sites around town, picks up things from colleagues and friends, and from everyday life in a Chinese community, as this Englishman did:

> *New avenues of opportunity in our lives have*
> *arisen more because of being in a Chinese society,*
> *than due to our marriage. I have learned largely*
> *how Chinese people live through my work and*
> *friends, rather than through my Chinese wife.*

~ ~ ~

I don't know about new avenues of opportunity!
As I was educated first in an Anglican missionary
school and then in England, my marriage to
an Englishman didn't open up any cultural
doors that weren't already open to me. Here in
Hong Kong, in the domestic sphere, my ability
to speak Cantonese means that I always deal
with workmen, plumbers, electricians, parking
attendants and policemen. I'm afraid these are
contacts I would rather not have!

Another husband seems to sympathise with her position:

In a cross-cultural marriage, a decision frequently
has to be made as to which culture to become
part of. This will obviously affect one partner
more than the other. As the 'outsider', I believe I
have taken good advantage of the opportunities
and have no regrets about being here. My life is
richer as a result. I do think, however, I should
have made a much greater effort to improve my
local language skills.

A Hong Kong Chinese professor who has lived in the
United States for many years wrote:

Certainly I would say I have become a lot more
Americanised. I have made many American friends
through my husband whom I would not have met
on my own. Also, I have become more direct and
outspoken, and my spoken English has become more
colloquial. But, my husband has not become more
sinicised. He eats very authentic Chinese food down

to snake soup, he loves it, but that's the extent.

The long workday of Hong Kong life seems to have limited the time and energy available for several European respondents to interface with Chinese culture. Although this American man speaks fluent Mandarin, and has a good working knowledge of written Chinese as well as of the culture and customs, he still feels he could have learned and experienced more.

> *Goodness no.* [I have not taken advantage of all the opportunities.] *In our lives we have barely skimmed the surface. The post-war work ethic of Hong Kong at least up to the mid 1980s meant that husband and wife both worked and were slaves to their respective jobs. There was not a lot of time to explore consciously each other's culture, unless one's spouse was lucky enough to have a position dealing exclusively with China, Europe or the United States. That we did not do more, I am sure, will be a regret when all is said and done.*

Some respondents in our survey have devoted much of their time to 'things Chinese'. On a practical level, knowledge of Chinese culture made it easier for one teacher to get employment, she said, with certainty. Several Western spouses have written and lectured extensively about Chinese customs, culture and history, and have served as active members of the Royal Asiatic Society or similar Asian cultural organisations. One Westerner has been described as 'more of a Hong Kong person than lots of local people' (*E-Journal on Hong Kong*

Cultural and Social Studies, 2002:415). Another, who has a good working knowledge of Cantonese, is considered to be an international authority on Hong Kong history and indeed aspects of the history of South China as well. This American woman has immersed herself:

> *I speak Cantonese fluently, and have learned so much about Chinese culture from my very old and honourable Cantonese teacher, Mr Tung, who taught me many of the 'whys' and 'wherefores' about this fascinating Chinese culture. In addition, I read a lot of books about, and by, Chinese people.*

Many of the families in our survey say they too have benefited, often wonderfully, from the breadth of experience of their Chinese and Western, and then Eurasian worlds. Through their different life choices, they have developed a deeper understanding of their homelands, their cultures and of themselves, both as individual family members, and altogether as a family unit. For many spouses and their children, Hong Kong has been a community conducive to exploration and growth, with its 'interesting and comprehensive culture' – a rich blend of the contemporary and the historic, and of both ancient Chinese traditions and more recent Western habits and customs.

Yet, with its inflexibilities, restrictions and legal responsibilities, the institution of marriage does not attract everyone, and a cross-cultural marriage can require even more compromises. A union between a Westerner and a Chinese, people whose cultures developed on opposite sides of the world, can bring a considerable amount of 'work' including communication sometimes in a second or third language, negotiations with in-laws from a generation often very culturally different, decisions about diet, religion, residence, lifestyle, and on top of this, dealing with various types of discrimination, subtle or blatant.

Yet there is joy, and much love. With hard work can come great satisfaction and pleasure. In essence, many of the wives and husbands I have talked with feel blessed to have shared their love and their lives with someone from another culture. They sense an expansion in their minds, souls, and hearts. 'I would not have lived the way I have, or been the person I have become' and 'We think a mixed marriage makes for a more interesting life, and our children also enjoy being Eurasian' express the general consensus of contentedness. An American Caucasian lady wrote:

> *'I would like to end my questionnaire by writing*
> [that] *being in a cross-cultural marriage has*
> *mostly been a wonderful opportunity for me*
> *to learn to grow in understanding myself, and*
> *others. Of course, over the years there have been*
> *frustrations from time to time. However, if I could*
> *live my life up to now over again, I would not*
> *change a single thing. It has all been an adventure,*
> *and I would do it all again in a second.'*

appendix A

Questions in the survey or asked at the interviews:

Question One
Did you or your partner hold any views before you met, or did you previously have any inkling that you might marry outside your own race?

Question Two
What languages are spoken between spouses and within the family?

Question Three
Have any misunderstandings with your spouse been caused by language difficulties?

Question Four
Have any misunderstandings been caused between you and your spouse by actions or body language?

Question Five
What food do you as a cross-cultural married couple and your family eat?

Question Six
Does your partner have any habits or customs, from his or her own culture, which you find amusing or annoying?

Question Seven
Are there any problems in relating to, or communicating with, in-laws?

Question Eight
Are there any problems in relating to, communicating with, or getting along with your spouse's friends?

Question Nine

What lifestyle do you and your Western-Chinese family lead? Do you visit family graves at Ching Ming? Do you and your family pay regard to *feng shui* and other Chinese as well as Western customs?

Question Ten

Where do you expect to live on retirement?

Question Eleven

Do you believe it is easier for a Western-Chinese marriage to be happier within a Chinese community, in a place like Singapore, Taiwan or Hong Kong, as opposed to living in a totally Western environment?

Question Twelve

Do you believe there is just as much chance of a cross-cultural marriage being successful and happy compared to a marriage with two partners from the same culture? Or do you believe that two people from different cultures is yet another 'hurdle' that has to be overcome?

Question Thirteen

Have you ever been discriminated against or looked down upon because of your Western-Chinese marriage?

Question Fourteen

Within a cross-cultural marriage, whole new avenues of opportunities open up regarding customs, culture, language, meeting new people, and so on. Would you say you have taken full advantage of such opportunities?

Question Fifteen

Is there anything else you feel is important that you would like to mention regarding cross-cultural marriages?

appendix B

Backgrounds of the 81 couples in the survey

Table One

Nationalities of the Westerners

British	Irish	New Zealand	Australian
53	1	2	2

USA	Canadian	German	Austrian
8	3	6	1

French	Polish	Swedish	Swiss
2	1	1	1

Note: No similar details are available for Chinese spouses, for men or women. Some were born in Mainland China and later moved to Hong Kong or elsewhere at some stage in their life. Others were born in Hong Kong and still live there, or have moved to another country. A small number of spouses are overseas Chinese, born in Cambodia or Britain, or elsewhere. Chinese spouses' natal families would have their origins in China, if not recently, a few generations ago.

Table Two

Place of Residence

Hong Kong	Britain	USA
57	14	4

Mainland China	Australia	Canada
2	2	2

Note: Many of the couples currently living in Hong Kong do travel a great deal, and many spend a considerable amount of time residing elsewhere.

Questionnaire Completion

In most cases, only one spouse filled in the questionnaire, either the husband or the wife, assisted by their partner to varying degrees.

In two cases, both spouses filled in a separate questionnaire.

As far as is known, twelve spouses filled in the questionnaire or were interviewed on their own. This is because the spouses were divorced, widowed or because they were not sure, so they told me, how their partners would react if asked to provide details of their marriage. Because they felt their spouse might object to their taking part in the survey, they preferred to keep quiet about it and participate independently.

As a general statement and as far as is known, with couples consisting of Chinese husbands and Western wives, it seemed that in most, but not all cases, the Western wife did the actual filling in of the questionnaire assisted, in most cases, by her spouse. This may explain why, among all four types of spouse, there are the fewest number of direct quotations attributed to Chinese men; often, the Western wife is 'speaking' on his or their behalf.

Table Three

Pairing of 81 Couples

82%	Marriages between a Western husband and a Chinese wife
18%	Marriages between a Western wife and a Chinese husband

Ages

This is a delicate topic on which a number of people, women especially, prefer to keep silent. In our survey, known or estimated ages of spouses ranged from their thirties to their mid-eighties. Most however were in their forties, fifties or sixties.

Husbands' Occupations

The following are broad classifications into which husbands' occupations fall. It can be seen that all husbands are generally well qualified and may be described as middle class.

As mentioned above, eighteen per cent of husbands are Chinese.

Two husbands stated they were retired. On 15 survey forms, the appropriate space was left blank, probably because they were retired from full time employment. Some respondents, nevertheless, work part-time or as volunteers in community service.

2	Architect	1	Hotelier
1	Business Consultant	1	Interpreter
12	Businessman/Manager	1	Journalist
2	Chartered Accountant	3	Lawyer
1	Chartered Surveyor	2	Medical Doctor
11	Civil Servant	1	Pharmacist
1	Curator	5	Police Officer
10	Educator	17	Retired or Assumed Retired
7	Engineer	1	Scientist (University Teacher)
1	Ex-Soldier	1	Tour Guide

Wives' Occupations

These are the broad classifications into which the wives' occupations fall. Again, it can be seen that, in the main, the wives, like their husbands, are well qualified, holding down responsible positions.

Eighteen per cent of wives are Westerners.

1	Accountant	5	Housewife
1	Beauty Therapist	1	Insurance Executive
11	Businesswoman / Manager	2	Lawyer
1	Chartered Secretary	1	Librarian
1	Chartered Surveyor	3	Nurse
1	Civil Engineer	1	Personal Secretary
2	Civil Servant	2	Police Officer
1	Dentist	1	Real Estate Executive
16	Educator	1	Restaurateur
1	Financial Analyst	2	Retired or Assumed Retired
1	Hairdresser	1	Social Worker
1	Hospital Administrator	1	Waitress
2	Hotelier	1	Writer

* 19 forms left blank

Table Four

Year(s) when Married

From	1946 to 1959	1960s	1970s	1980s	1990s	2000
	4	18	27	22	22	7

Total = 100 per cent

Table Five

Number of Children

Nil	One	Two	Three	Four
34	14	37	13	2

Total = 100 per cent

appendix C

One Hong Kong-based British-Chinese couple, who filled in their questionnaire together, returned it with this list of friends and acquaintances in interracial marriages. They said these 28 couples share common traits: 'open-minded, outward looking, and of above average education.'

The husband's ethnicity is listed first.

1   British and Filipina
2   British and Taiwanese
3   French and Taiwanese
4   French and Macau Chinese
5   French and Japanese
6   British and Japanese
7   American and Japanese
8   British and Afghan
9   British and Indian
10 British and Hong Kong Eurasian
11 New Zealand and Hong Kong Eurasian
12 New Zealand and Hong Kong Chinese
13 Hong Kong Eurasian and American
14 British and American Chinese
15 American and Mainland Chinese
16 Belgian and Mainland Chinese émigre to Belgium
17 British and Mainland Chinese
18 British and Korean
19 Malaysian Chinese and Australian
20 Australian and Hong Kong Chinese
21 Austrian and Shanghainese émigre
22 Hong Kong Chinese and English
23 American and American Chinese
24 British and Vietnamese Chinese
25 Polish and Hong Kong Eurasian
26 French and Filipina
27 German and Thai
28 British and Thai

glossary

amah
媽姐

Female domestic helper, usually referring to a Chinese.

cheung saam
長衫

For women, a long sheath-like dress with high Mandarin collar and splits up both sides, of varying length, to allow for leg movement. For men, a long, loose-fitting gown.

chi
(hei in Cantonese)
氣

A complex word similar to the Greek pneuma or the Yoga prana, meaning 'life force.' It pervades everything including mind-body organisms.

chinglish

A mixture of Chinese and English words often used together in the same sentence.

Ching Ming
清明

A spring time festival, sometimes dubbed the 'Chinese Easter,' when visits are paid to family graves, they are swept and tidied. Usually falls on the 5th of April.

Chung Yeung
重陽

A festival held on the ninth day of the Ninth Moon when families climb hills and vantage points to seek protection from future disasters. Graves are often swept on the same day.

compradore
買辦

A Chinese or Eurasian, who worked in a *hong* spoke both Chinese and English, and was reasonably at home in both cultures. He acted as a middleman for business transactions between the races. A term also used, years ago, to mean a Chinese grocer.

concubine 妾侍	A secondary wife who had her proper place within the Chinese family and within Chinese society. A law was enacted in Hong Kong, in October 1971, prohibiting Chinese males from taking new concubines from then on. A few elderly ones still exist.
congee 粥	Rice gruel.
divining blocks 問杯	A pair of small timber blocks found in temples and used for asking the gods questions. They are tossed up and, depending on which way they land, flat or rounded side up, the answer is interpreted as 'yes', 'no' or 'the gods are laughing at the question!'
downhomer	The term for a temporary wife. Having such a wife was a custom common among members of the British armed forces in places like Hong Kong before World War Two.
face 面子	A complex word meaning prestige, reputation, dignity, honour, self-respect or status.
feng shui (fung shui) 風水	The principle that buildings, graves, the work place and so on should be aligned so that they 'reconcile' with environmental 'currents' and cosmic principles.
gwailo 鬼佬	Literally translated as 'ghost person' but often loosely translated as 'foreign devil'. Strictly speaking, it refers to a Western man.
gwaipor 鬼婆	Literally translated as 'ghost woman', for a Western woman.

Hakka 客家	(literally meaning 'guest family') Over the centuries, the Hakka Chinese moved from the north to the south of China in waves. They have their own customs and cuisine. Their women did not bind their feet.
hong 行	Large business house or commercial enterprise.
kit fat 結髮	The principal Chinese wife, dating back to the days when polygamous marriages were common.
Kowloon 九龍	Literally meaning 'nine dragons,' signifying nine foothills. Kowloon is situated on the mainland side of Hong Kong.
kow tow 叩頭	Kneeling, bending forward, and then touching the forehead to the floor a given number of times. This is done by one person to pay his or her respects to a more senior person. It is still sometimes done by children to parents and grandparents on their birthdays or at the Lunar New Year.
lai see 利是	'Lucky money' usually presented as a gift in special red envelopes.
Mandarin 國語	The Peking dialect, originally the language of the ruling classes.
memsahib	Originally an Indian term of respect for a European woman, but sometime used in fun in other parts of the East when talking about European women or, more especially, when men talk about their wives.

Nanyang 南洋	Those who emigrated to parts of south-east or southern Asia.
New Territories 新界	Hong Kong's 'hinterland', that is to say, North of Boundary Street, which was leased by China to Britain in 1898, for 99 years. This, together with the remainder of Hong Kong, was returned by Britain to China in 1997. Parts of the New Territories and outlying islands are still very rural and wooded, yet very few farmers remain.
protected woman	Common in places like Hong Kong up to World War Two when Western-Chinese marriages were not acceptable in polite society. Protected Chinese women, who were the mistresses of Western men, were given a 'certificate' so that, if they were stopped in the street by police they could prove they were 'respectable' and not prostitutes.
Putonghua 普通話	The present day standard national language of the People's Republic of China based largely on Mandarin.
sam foo 衫褲	Chinese style trousers and jacket. Also worn by women as a form of 'trouser-suit.'
sampan 舢舨	A small boat usually sculled, directly translated in Cantonese as 'three planks'.
taipan 大班	Meaning 'big boss', usually referring to the head of a large Western *hong* or company.
Tanka 蜑家	This term refers to the largest sub-ethnic group of boat people in Hong Kong. Traditionally they are born, live and die on their boats. They

earn their living by fishing, and other pursuits on the water, although in more recent years many have found employment ashore. In the nineteenth century in Hong Kong, many Tanka women who did not bind their feet, sometimes known as 'saltwater girls', they became the Westerners 'protected women' [kept women].

tin fong
填房

Literally means 'fill the room' and refers to a wife who has been taken after the first wife has died.

tsip tsi
妾侍

A concubine or secondary wife.

Tung Sing
(Tong Sing)
通勝

The Chinese Almanac published annually containing, among other things, weather information, horoscopes and guides for choosing auspicious dates to carry out certain tasks, such as moving house or getting married.

yin and yang
陰陽

Basic cosmic, dualistic, negative and positive principles which apply to countless 'pairs', like man and woman, light and darkness, and odd and even numbers. These pairs all complement rather than compete with each other.

bibliography

This bibliography lists all publications, together with a few unpublished papers, which are mentioned in the text. Some other works are also listed which may be of interest to anyone who wishes to explore further the subject of cross-cultural marriages:

Akers-Jones, David, 'Report on a Visit to San Tin Village Complex,' *Aspects of Social Organization in the New Territories*, 9-10 May 1964, Royal Asiatic Society Hong Kong Branch, week-end symposium, 1964.

Alibhai-Brown, Yasmin, *Mixed Feelings, The Complex Lives of Mixed Race Britons*, UK, The Women's Press Ltd, 2001.

'That Racial Mix', Hong Kong, *The Asia Magazine*, July 27, 1986.

Baker, Barbara, *Chinese Ink, Western Pen-Stories of China*, New York, Oxford University Press, 2000.

Baker, Hugh, 'The Five Great Clans of the New Territories,' *Journal of the Hong Kong Branch of the Royal Asiatic Society*, Vol. 6, pp.25-47, 1966.

Ball, J Dyer, *Things Chinese, or Notes Connected with China*, Singapore, republished 1989 by Graham Brash, 1903.

Bard, Solomon , 'Obituary: K.M.A. Barnett OBE,' *Journal of the Hong Kong Branch of the Royal Asiatic Society*, vol. 27, 1987.

———— , *Traders of Hong Kong: Some Foreign Merchant Houses 1841-1899*, Hong Kong, Urban Council Hong Kong, 1993.

Barnett, K.M.A., 'Hong Kong Before the Chinese, the Frame, the Puzzle and the Missing Pieces,' *Journal of the Hong Kong Branch of the Royal Asiatic Society*, vol. 4., 1964

———— 'Removing Some Barriers to Comprehension, a New Look at Cantonese Expletives,' *Journal of the Hong Kong Branch of the Royal Asiatic Society*, vol. 10, 1970.

———— , 'Do Words from Pre-Chinese Languages Survive in Hong Kong?' *Journal of the Hong Kong Branch of the Royal Asiatic Society*, vol. 14, 1974.

Bentley, Man Wah Leung, 'Remembrance of Times Past: the University and Chungking,' *Dispersal and Renewal, Hong Kong University During the War Years*, eds. Clifford Mathews and Oswald Cheung, Hong Kong, Hong Kong

University Press, 1998.

'The Best Lovers East or West', *Sunday Morning Post*, Agenda, Hong Kong, March 20, 1994.

Bickers, Robert, Empire Made Me, *An Englishman Adrift in Shanghai*, UK, Allen Lane an imprint of Penguin Books, 2003.

Bickley, Gillian, *The Golden Needle, The Biography of Frederick Stewart (1836-1889)*, Hong Kong, David C. Lam Institute for East-West Studies, Hong Kong Baptist University, 1997.

————, *Court in Time: A Magistrate's Court in Nineteenth Century Hong Kong*, Hong Kong, Proverse Press, 2005.

Block, Alex Ben, *The Legend of Bruce Lee*, New York, Del Publishing Co, 1974.

Borralho, Leonel, '*Macanese Patois in Poetry*', Hong Kong, *Hong Kong Standard*, January 23, 1984.

Brown, Graham, 'Love Affair Between Black and White Scandalises South African Town, Hong Kong, *South China Morning Post*, February 3, 1988.

Bruce, Phillip, 'What it was Really Like,' *Hong Kong Military History Notes*, issue seven, Hong Kong, Phillip Bruce, October 1987.

———— , 'The Angels of Wanchai', *History Notes 1*, Hong Kong, Phillip Bruce, Mid-1990.

Buck, Pearl S., *The Good Earth*, New York, Pocket Books Inc, 1931.

———— , *Letter From Peking*, UK, Methuen, 1957.

Burton, Michael James, *Interracial Marriage in Hong Kong*, M.Phil. thesis, Hong Kong, University of Hong Kong, 1992.

Cameron, Nigel, *An Illustrated History of Hong Kong*, Hong Kong, Oxford University Press, 1991.

Chan, Mimi, *Images of Chinese Women in Anglo-Chinese Literature*, Hong Kong, Joint Publishing, 1989.

Chan Sui-jeung, *The Jews in Kaifeng, Reflections on Sino-Judiac History*, Hong Kong, Hong Kong Jewish Chronicle, 1986.

Chang, Michael, with Mike Yorkey, *Holding Serve – Persevering on and off the Court*, New York, Hodder and Stoughton, 2002.

Cheng, Irene, *Intercultural Reminiscences,* David C. Lam Institute for East-West Studies, Hong Kong, Hong Kong Baptist University, 1997.

Chiu, Vivian, 'Wedded to the World of Arranged Marriages,' Hong Kong, *South China Morning Post*, June 2, 1992.

Choa, G. H., *The Life and Times of Sir Kai Ho Kai, A Prominent Figure in Nineteenth-Century Hong Kong*, revised 2000, Hong Kong, the Chinese University of Hong Kong Press, 1981.

Chong, Dennis 'Red-light rethink,' *The Standard*, Hong Kong, June 23, 2003.

Clark, Russell S., *An End to Tears*, Sydney, Bridge Printery, 1946.

Clarke, Judith, 'Reminder of a Life Left Behind', *South China Morning Post*, Hong Kong, May 26, 2001.

Clavell, James, *Taipan*, USA, the Philadelphia Coronet Books, 1984.

Coates, Austin, *City of Broken Promises*, Hong Kong, Heinemann Asia, 1967.

————— , *Myself a Mandarin, Memoirs of a Special Magistrate*, Heinemann Asia, 1968.

Coates, P. D., *The China Consuls*, Oxford University Press, 1988.

Cooper, Anthony G., *The Sanctuary*, Hong Kong, Communications Management Ltd, 1984.

Crabb, C. H., *Malaya's Eurasians – An Opinion*, Singapore, Eastern Universities Press, 1960.

Dalrymple, William, *White Mughals*, Harper Collins, 2002.

Davies, Derek, 'Obituary: KMA Barnett OBE.' *Journal of the Hong Kong Branch of the Royal Asiatic Society*, vol. 27, 1987.

Davis, Leonard, 'The Twain Can Meet and Live Happily Ever After,' *Sunday Standard*, Hong Kong, October 17, 1993.

Dawson, R., *The Chinese Chameleon: An Analysis of European Conceptions of Chinese Civilisation*, UK, Oxford University Press, 1967.

Edwards, Jack, *Banzai You Bastards!*, Hong Kong, Corporate Communications, undated.

Eitel, E. J., *Europe in China*, reprint, Hong Kong, Hong Kong University Press, 1983.

E-Journal on Hong Kong Cultural and Social Studies, printed edition, chief editor Elizabeth Sinn, Centre of Asian Studies Hong Kong University, vol. 1, 2002.

Elliott, Helen, 'Return to the Fold for Woman in Red', *South China Morning Post*, Hong Kong, February 8, 2003.

Endacott, G. B., *A History of Hong Kong*, UK, Oxford University Press, 1958.

'*The Eurasian: A New Image*', *The Asia Magazine*, *passim*, November 22, 1964, .

Evans, T. G., 'It Takes Time to Know the Chinese', *Hong Kong Standard*, letter to the editor, February 6, 1984.

Far East Expatriate, 'Mixed and Maybe Shaken – But Most Definitely Not Stirred.', March 1987.

Feign, Larry, *The World of Lilly Wong, A Far-eastern Cross-cultural Cartoon Love Story*, Hambalan Press Hong Kong, first published by Macmillan Publishing (HK), 1988, 1993.

————— , *Hong Kong Fairy Tales*, Hong Kong, Hambalan Press, 1994.

Fenton, Anna, 'Shock All Expats are Sure to Share,' *South China Morning Post*, Hong Kong, October 6, 1991.

Fisher, Stephen Frederick, *Eurasians in Hong Kong, a Sociological Study of a Marginal Group*, Hong Kong, Hong Kong University M.Phil. thesis, 1975.

Fong, Bernard, 'Index Finger Pointed at our Monetary Chief', *South China Morning Post*, Hong Kong, November 14, 1987.

Fong, Colleen and Judy Yung, 'In Search of the Right Spouse: Interracial Marriage among Chinese and Japanese Americans'. *Amerasia Journal* 21:3, 77-98, USA, winter 1995/96.

Free China Review, vol. 41, No. 12, passim, December 1991.

Fu, Charlene, 'Jewish Remnant Resist Assimilation', *Hong Kong Standard*, August 16, 1990.

Garrett, Valery M., *Heaven is High the Emperor Far Away: Merchants and Mandarins in Old Canton*, Oxford University Press, 2002.

Gaw, Kenneth, *Superior Servants, The Legendary Cantonese Amahs of the Far East*, Oxford University Press, 1988.

Gillingham, Paul, *At the Peak, Hong Kong Between the Wars,* Hong Kong, Macmillan, 1983.

Go, Simon, *Hong Kong Apothecary, A Visual History of Chinese Medicine Packaging*, Hong Kong, MCCM Creations, 2003.

Gomes, Authur E., *Newsletter Hong Kong Prisoners of War Association*, front cover, Hong Kong, 2003.

Gray, John, *Men are from Mars, Women are from Venus*, UK, Thorsons, 1993.

Gupta, Kanta, *Living Together and Concubinage: A Cross-cultural Study*, an unpublished paper, mid-1990s.

Hacker, Arthur, *The Hong Kong Visitors Book, A Historical Who's Who*, Hong Kong, The Guidebook Company, 1997.

Hall, Peter, *In The Web*, Peter Hall, 1992.

Han, Stephanie, 'When is Daddy Coming Home?' *Post Magazine*, Hong Kong, April 14, 2002.

Han Suyin, *A Many Splendoured Thing*, Jonathan Cape, 1852.

Hayes, James, 'Obituary: KMA Barnett OBE,' *Journal of the Hong Kong Branch of the Royal Asiatic Society*, vol. 27, 1987.

Hetherington, John, 'Hard Work Taking a Toll on Marriages Warn Experts,' *Hong Kong Standard*, Hong Kong, June 21, 1990.

Hilditch, Tom, 'SAR,' *South China Morning Post*, Hong Kong, 2003, May, 13.

Hoe, Susanna, *The Private Life of Old Hong Kong, Western Women in the British Colony 1841-1941*, New York, Oxford University Press, 1991.

Holdsworth, May, *Foreign Devils, Expatriates in Hong Kong*, New York, Oxford University Press, 2002.

Hong Kong 1971, Hong Kong Public Records Office, 'Question of European Inspectorate - Police Department ...marrying ladies of not pure European descent', Hong Kong Government minutes, 'Depts/Inspectorate – Police Department, 1681/47.', 1947. Hong Kong Government, 1972.

Hong Kong Standard, 'Shanghai Refugee is King of the Sea.', April 28, 1989.

Hong Kong Standard, 'Judaism is Just a Memory.', August 9, 1990.

Hughes, Owen, 'Chronicle of a Hong Kong Dynasty', *South China Morning Post*, Hong Kong, September 13, 1992.

————— , 'Shaw Business,' *South China Morning Post Magazine*, Hong Kong, March 27, 1994.

Hughes, Richard, *Borrowed Place Borrowed Time, Hong Kong and its Many Faces*. UK, Andre Deutsch, 1968.

Identity and Choice, Cross-Cultural Marriage, eds Rosemary Breger and Rosanna Hill, New York, Oxford, 1998.

Immigration Department Hong Kong Government, letter from Director to author together with enclosures: pamphlet, *How to Apply (for) Marriage Registration*, specimen marriage certificates, August 13, 2003.

Ingrams, Harold, *Hong Kong*, UK, Her Majesty's Stationary Office, 1952.

Jameson, Gardner and Elliott Williams, *The Drinking Man's Diet*, Hong Kong, Far East American Publishing Co. Ltd., 1964.

Jen-siu, Michael, 'China is Falling Head Over Heels for Valentine's Day', *South China Morning Post*, Hong Kong, February 15, 2003.

Karlgren, Bernhard, *Sound and Symbol in Chinese*, Hong Kong, Hong Kong University Press, 1923, reprinted 1971.

King, Elaine, '...Alias Jimmy McWong', *M Magazine*, Hong Kong, (c. 1996).

Kuriansky, Judy, 'For Better or Worse', ed. Anna Healy Fenton, *South China Morning Post*, Hong Kong, May 26, 2002.

Lacroix, Karl and David Marriott, *How to Marry a Western Man* (published in Chinese), 2003.

Lai, T. C., Husein Rofe, Philip Man, *Things Chinese*, Hong Kong, Swindon Book Company, 1971.

Lai, T. C., *Chinese Food for Thought*, Hong Kong, Hong Kong Book Centre, 1978.

Lee, Elaine, 'Single Minded', ed. Anna Healy Fenton, *South China Morning Post*, Hong Kong, December 8, 2002.

Lee, Linda, *The Bruce Lee Story*, Santa Clarita, California, Chara Publications Inc, USA, 1989.

Lee, Vicky, *Being Eurasian, Memories Across Racial Divides*, Hong Kong, Hong Kong University Press, 2004.

Lethbridge, Henry J., 'The Best of Both Worlds,' F*ar Eastern Economic Review*, pp. 128-130, Hong Kong, October 10, 1968.

Ling Huping, 'Family and Marriage of Late-Nineteenth and Early-Twentieth Century Chinese Immigrant Women', *Journal of American Ethnic History*, Winter 2000.

Little, Alicia Helen S., 'A Millionaire's Courtship,' *Macao: Mysterious Decay and Romance*, Oxford University Press, 1997.

Lowenstein, Merrill, memorandum from State Library of Victoria, Australia, to author regarding inter-racial marriage in Australia, May 26, 2005.

Luk Kwok Hotel, *The Redeveloped Luk Kwok Hotel*, Press release by the Hotel, undated.

Macartney, Sir H, 'On Anglo-Chinese Marriages,' *History of the Laws, Etc., of Hong Kong.*, 1898.

Maher, Virginia, 'A Life Less Ordinary', *South China Morning Post*, Hong Kong, January 4, 2003.

————, 'Past Lives: David Hampton,' *South China Morning Post*, Hong Kong, April 7, 2003.

Mahoney, Dino, 'Screen Goddess Who Danced to a Jazzier Score, Classical Notes,' *South China Morning Post*, Hong Kong, April 4, 2004.

Maisel, Richard and Caroline Hodges Persell, *How Sampling Works*, Thousand Oaks, California, USA, Pine Forge Press, 1996.

Mason, Richard, *The World of Suzie Wong*, Fontana, 1957.

Matchett, Barbara, 'How Lalu Became Polly – And Helped Build America', *South China Morning Post,* Hong Kong, December 3, 1981 .

Maugham, W Somerset, *The Complete Short Stories of W. Somerset Maugham,* William Heinemann, 1951.

McCord, Mark, 'No place to call home,' *South China Morning Post*, Hong Kong, July 23, 2000.

McCunn, Ruthanne Lum, *An Illustrated History of the Chinese in America,* USA, Design Enterprises of San Francisco, 1979.

————— , *A Thousand Pieces of Gold*, USA, Design Enterprises of San Francisco, 1981.

—————, *Chinese American Portraits, Personal Histories 1828-1988*, USA, Chronicle Books, 1988.

Merson, J, *The Genius that was China: East and West in the Making of the Modern World*, New York, The Overlook Press, 1990.

Methold, K. and D. D. [Dan] Waters, *Understanding Technical English*, vol 1, 2 and 3, Longman Group, first published 1973.

Minchin, James, *No Man is an Island: A Study of Singapore's Lee Kuan Yew*, Allen and Unwin, 1986.

Mixed Marriages in the New Territories, video call no. Radio Hong Kong 16547, Hong Kong University Main Library, 1983.

Mo, Timothy, *Sour Sweet*, UK, Sphere Books Ltd., 1982.

Morris, Jan, *Hong Kong Xianggong*, Penguin, 1988.

Needham, Joseph *et al*, a series of volumes of varying dates titled, *Science and Civilisation in China*, UK, Cambridge University Press.

Ng, James, 'Mixed Marriage' Volume Two, *Windows on a Chinese Past*, Otago Heritage Books New Zealand (total four volumes), 1995.

Nicol, Jean, 'Marital Blues: Don't Worry, it Gets Better,' *South China Morning Post*, Hong Kong, February 14, 2003.

—————, 'Confucianism – The Root of Hong Kong's Search for Wealth,' *South China Morning Post*, Hong Kong, May 30, 2003.

—————, 'Reading Emotions,' *South China Morning Post*,' Hong Kong, March 12, 2004.

Pakenham, Valery, *The Noonday Sun*, Edwardians in the tropics, Methuen London Ltd., 1985.

Paley, Edward, 'Behind the Jewish Renaissance,' *South China Morning Post*, Hong Kong, 1993, April 18.

Parker, David, *Through Different Eyes: The Cultural Identities of Young Chinese People in Britain*, Ashgate Publishing UK, 1995.

Parry, Hazel, 'Forbidden Love Endures Test of Time', *South China Morning Post*, Hong Kong, December 2, 2002.

Parry, Hazel, 'Love Story Catches Top Director's Eye', *South China Morning Post*, Hong Kong, December 16, 2002.

Parry, Jane, 'Feminist Author Attacks Stereotypes', *Hong Kong Standard*, Profile, November 28, 1989.

Pastor, 'Did God Want Chinese and Europeans to intermarry?' *Newsletter, St Joseph's Catholic Church*, Garden Road, Hong Kong, mid-1990s.

Paxman, Jeremy, *The English: A Portrait of a People*, Michael Joseph, 1998.

Pittis, Donald and Susan J. Henders, *Macao: Mysterious Decay and Romance*, UK, Oxford University Press, 1997.

Pollock, David C. and Ruth E. VanReken, *The Third Culture Kid Experience: Growing Up Among Worlds*, Intercultural Press USA, 1999.

Reid, Margaret, 'Love and Marriage,' ed. Maggie Keswick, *The Thistle and the Jade, A Celebration of 150 Years of Jardine Matheson & Co*, UK, Octopus, 1982.

Ricketts, Harry, *People Like Us: Sketches of Hong Kong*, Hong Kong, Eurasia Publishing Corporation, 1977.

Roland, Charles G., *Long Night's Journey into Day: Prisoners of War in Hong Kong and Japan, 1941-1945*, Canada, Wilfred Laurier University Press, 2001.

Romano, Dugan, *Intercultural Marriage, Promises and Pitfalls*, Intercultural Press, USA, 3rd edition, first published 1988, 2001.

Schultz, Duane, *The Maverick War: Chennault and the Flying Tigers*, New York, St. Martin's Press, 1987.

Selby, Anne and Stephen, 'China Coast Pidgin English,' *Journal of the Hong Kong Branch of the Royal Asiatic Society*, vol. 35, 1997.

Sharp, Ilsa, 'The Choi Factor', *South China Morning Post*, Hong Kong, April 26, 2001.

Shaw, Traute, 'Becoming Part of this Great City Hong Kong,' *Servus Hong Kong, Austria in and Around the Pearl of the Orient, a Visual Random Walk down History and Memory Lane by the Austrian-Hong Kong Community with some Stewardship of Gordian Gaeta*, Hong Kong, MCCM Creations, 2004.

Simmons, Ruth, 'Only With Civility Will Globalisation Work', *South China Morning Post*, Hong Kong, January 21, 2003.

Sinclair, Kevin, 'Tribute to Anne Hughes, a Dear Friend of Hong Kong', *Hong Kong Standard*, Hong Kong, April 11, 1988.

Slavick, Madeleine Marie and Barbara Baker, *Round – Poems and Photographs of Asia*, Hong Kong, Asia 2000 Ltd, 1998.

Slavick, Madeleine Marie, *delicate access*, Hong Kong, Sixth Finger Press, 2004.

Smith, Carl T., *Chinese Christians: Elites,Middlemen and the Church in Hong Kong*, Hong Kong, Oxford University Press, 1985.

———— , 'Ng Akew, One of Hong Kong's Protected Women', *A Sense of History, Studies in the Social and Urban History of Hong Kong*, Hong Kong, Hong Kong Educational Publishing Co., 1995.

Snow, Phillip, *The Fall of Hong Kong: Britain, China and the Japanese Occupation*, Yale University Press, 2003.

Sohmen, Helmut, 'Global Shipping – An Austrian-Hong Kong Symbiosis,' *Servus Hong Kong*, Hong Kong, MCCM Creations, 2004.

South China Morning Post, 'Human Eatery Boobs.' Hong Kong, 2003.

South China Morning Post, '75pc of HK firms employ women in senior management,' Hong Kong, February 23, 2004.

Spurr, Russell, 'Filing a Colourful Exclusive', *Sunday Morning Post*, Hong Kong, August 14, 1988.

———— , *Excellency, the Governors of Hong Kong*, Hong Kong, FormAsia Hong Kong, 1995.

Sung, Betty Lee, *Chinese American Intermarriage, Center for Migration Studies*, New York, 1990.

Tan, Amy, *The Kitchen God's Wife*, Winsor Chivers Press UK, 1991.

———— , *The Hundred Secret Senses*, Ivy Books New York, 1995.

Temple, Robert K G, *China, Land of Discovery and Invention*, Patrick Stevens, UK, Wellingborough, 1985.

Tomlinson, Peta, 'Tightrope Romance', *South China Morning Post*, Hong Kong, September 15, 2002.

Tongue, Ray and Dan Waters, 'English, HK-Style', *South China Morning Post*, Hong Kong, September 29, 1978.

Topley, Marjorie, 'Marriage Resistance in Rural Kwangtung,' *Women in Chinese Society*, eds Margery Wolf and Roxane Wiske, Stanford, California, USA, Stanford University Press, 1975.

Tryfos, Peter, *Sampling Methods for Applied Research: Text and Case*, J., UK, Carey Publishing Service, 1996.

Tse, Liu Frances, *Ho Kam-Tong, A Man for all Seasons*, ed. Frances McDonald, Hong Kong, Compradore House Ltd., 2003.

Tu, Andrew and Elsie, *Shouting at the Mountain, A Hong Kong Story of Love and Commitment*, South China Morning Post, Hong Kong. 2004.

Walbrook, Peter, 'Lost World of Suzie Wong,' *South China Morning Post*, Hong Kong, April 4, 2004.

Wallis, Belinda, 'Guess Who's Coming to Yam Cha?' *South China Morning Post*, Focus, Hong Kong, March 18, 1994.

Wan, Mariana, 'First Family,' *Sunday Morning Post*, Hong Kong, January 27, 1991.

Wang, Annie, 'People's Republic of Desire,' *South China Morning Post*, Hong Kong, February 25, 2004.

Waters, Dan, 'In the Steps of Lu Pan: Reminiscences of Building in Hong Kong', *Journal of the Hong Kong Branch of the Royal Asiatic Society*, vol. 29, 1991.

———— 'Hong Kong Hongs with Long Histories and British Connections,' *Journal of the Royal Asiatic Society*, vol. 30, 1993.

————, *21st Century Management: Keeping Ahead of the Japanese and Chinese*, Prentice Hall/Simon and Schuster, 1991.

————, 'Chinese Funerals: A Case Study', *Journal of the Hong Kong Branch of the Royal Asiatic Society*, vol. 31, 1996.

————, 'Taking a Godson,' *Journal of the Hong Kong Branch of the Royal Asiatic Society*, vol. 33, 1996.

————, 'Foreigners and Fung Shui,' *Journal of the Hong Kong Branch of the Royal Asiatic Society*', vol. 34, 1997.

————, *Faces of Hong Kong, An Old Hand's Reflections*, Prentice Hall/Simon and Schuster, 1995.

————, 'Laughter Across the Great Wall: A Comparison of Chinese and Western Humour', *Journal of the Hong Kong Branch of the Royal Asiatic Society*, vol. 38, 2000.

Watson, James L., 'From the Common Pot: Feasting with Equals in Chinese Society,' *Anthropos*, 82, USA., 1987.

Wei Peh T'i, Betty, 'Racism Rears its Ugly Head,' *South China Morning Post*, Hong Kong, September 27, 1981.

Welsh, Frank, *A History of Hong Kong*, Harper Collins, 1993.

Wen Chihua, 'The "We First" Generation,' *South China Morning Post*, Hong Kong, July 15, 2001.

'Why a Chinese girl says Western men are best', *South China Morning Post*, Hong Kong, March 19, 1994.

Wilkerson, Isabel, 'Mixed Marriages Hit a Nerve in the South', *South China Morning Post*, Hong Kong, December 3, 1991.

Windridge, Dr Charles, *Tong Sing, The Chinese Book of Wisdom, Based on the Ancient Chinese Almanac*, UK, Kyle Cathie Ltd, 1999.

Wolfendale, Stuart, 'Last Post for Charlie', *Sunday Morning Post Magazine*, Hong Kong, mid-1990s.

——————— , 'The Gweilos Who "Go Bush",' *Sunday Morning Post*, Hong Kong, 4 April, 1993.

Wong, Morrison G, 'A Look at Intermarriage Among the Chinese in the United States in 1980,' *Sociological Perspectives*, vol.32, No.1, pp.87-107, Pacific Sociological Association, USA, 1989.

Worboys, Kay, 'Who's With Who?' *Sunday Morning Post Magazine*, Hong Kong, February 12, 1995.

Wright, Michael, letter to author, September 5, 2002.

Wright-Nooth with Mark Adkin, *Prisoner of the Turnip Heads, Horror, Hunger and Humour in Hong Kong 1941-1945*, UK, Leo Cooper,1994.

Yung, Judy, *Chinese Women of America, A Pictorial History, Chinese Culture Foundation of San Francisco*, USA, University of Washington Press, 1986.

web sites

Lee, Bruce and Linda (nee Emery):
http://www.historylink.org/essays/output.cfm?file_id=3999

Maugham, W Somerset:
http://www.bl.uk/collections/british/modbrimaugh.html
http://www.nytimes.com/2004/03/14/books/review/14ALLENT.
html?ex=1116388800&en=04ff89c5fc468728&ei=5070

Mo, Timothy:
http://www.litencyc.com/php/speople.php?rec=true&UID=3144

Wong, Anna May:
http://www.pictureshowman.com/articles_personalities_wong.cfm

index

ONE COUPLE TWO CULTURES
81 Western-Chinese Couples Talk about Love and Marriage
By Dan Waters

Published by MCCM Creations 2005
Reprint edition 2008
info@mccmcreations.com
www.mccmcreations.com

Cover design & illustration: Peter Suart
Design & Artwork: Ng Ching-man, Cheng Wai-chung
Printing: Jade Productions

Customs/Culture
ISBN 978-988-97610-0-4